MW01127345

THE GULEN MOVEMENT

Turkey's Islamic Supremacist Cult and its Contributions to the Civilization Jihad

By Christopher Holton and Clare Lopez

CIVILIZATION JIHAD READER SERIES

Volume 8

Copyright © 2015

ISBN-13: 978-1522702221
ISBN-10: 1522702229

The Gulen Movement: Turkey's Islamic Supremacist Cult and Its contribution to the Civilization Jjihad in America is published in the United States by the Center for Security Policy Press, a division of the Center for Security Policy.

December 10, 2015

THE CENTER FOR SECURITY POLICY
1901 Pennsylvania Avenue, Suite 201 Washington, DC 20006
Phone: (202) 835-9077 | Email: info@securefreedom.org
For more information, please see securefreedom.org

Book design by Adam Savit and Brittany Clift
Cover design by Alex VanNess

TABLE OF CONTENTS

Foreword

In 2012, I had the opportunity to experience first-hand the mix of sophisticated influence operation and Islamic supremacism guised as Turkish nationalism that is practiced by the so-called Gulen Movement (GM). This organization has properly been described as a Muslim cult of personality. It is inspired and led by an expatriate Turk, Fethullah Gulen, who operates his multi-billion international education and business empire from an armed camp in Pennsylvania's Pocono Mountains.

Three years ago, a group dominated by Gulenists sought to establish a publicly supported charter high school focusing on science, technology, engineering and math (STEM) in Virginia's Loudoun County. Their controversial and deeply problematic proposal caused me and many other residents to become knowledgeable about Gulen's program and the more than 140 of his schools operating as of now across America – with a thousand more in Turkey and elsewhere around the world. Happily, in the end, faced with the intense and informed opposition of many Loudoun citizens and a charter school application with myriad flaws, the school board declined to approve the Loudoun County Math and Information Technology Academy.

That close encounter with a movement that has been infiltrating the U.S. school system and influencing our elected officials for many years not only illuminated for us at the Center for Security Policy the scope and import of the Gulen's operations in America. It also made plain the need to raise awareness among educators, school boards and administrators, students and their families and legislators about this little-known Turkish and Islamic supremacist cult and its reclusive leader, Fethullah Gulen.

In particular, as we delved deeper into the details concerning the Gulen Movement, it became obvious that the carefully-cultivated external image of harmony, "interfaith dialogue," and tolerance promoted by the Gulenists, in fact, masks a far more troubling agenda about Turkey, Islamic supremacism, and extending the dominion of its operating code, shariah. The vast network of schools and universities, established by the GM first in Turkey, then globally, touts a commitment to scholastic excellence in math and the sciences. But their graduates have infiltrated every level of the Turkish government and helped to destroy the secular legacy of Kemal Ataturk.

Abroad, including notably in the United States, GM-associated "cultural organizations" purported to tout Turkey's architecture, cuisine, dance, music, etc. These front groups actually served, however, as a vehicle for conducting influence operations against large numbers of Americans, some of them quite prominent, in order to advance a Turkish/Islamist ideological agenda. All-expenses-paid trips brought hundreds of civic and faith community leaders, city, county, state and federal lawmakers and their staff, school administrators and students to see the wonders of Turkey, but also ensured that they spent plenty of time while there with Gulenists and their friends.

In October 2015, *USA Today* gave front-page, above-the-fold treatment to such Gulenist influence operations, revealing that federal investigators had determined that Gulen Movement fronts paid for hundreds of trips to Turkey for members of the U.S. Congress and their staff while illegally concealing the actual source of that funding. In addition, the FBI and other federal agencies are investigating numerous other allegations of irregularities at GM charter schools across the country.

While much has been published about Gulen and his movement, the most revealing passages ultimately come not from investigative reporters or critics, but from Fethullah Gulen himself in a book he wrote in 1998: *Prophet Mohammed as Commander.* A concluding segment of this monograph quotes extensively from that work, because it is so revealing of Gulen's thinking about how jihad should be practiced against the "unbelievers" or infidels in countries like ours. The following passage is as illustrative as it should be alarming:

> ...[Muslim] believers should also equip themselves with the most sophisticated weaponry. Force has an important place in obtaining the desired result, so believers cannot be indifferent to it. Rather they must be much more advanced in science and technology than unbelievers so that they should not allow unbelievers to use "force" for their selfish benefit. According to Islam, "right is might"; so, in order to prevent might from being right in the hands of unbelievers and oppressors, believers must be mightier than others.

An Islamic state...should be able to secure peace and justice in the world and no power should have the courage to make corruption in any part of the earth. This will be possible when Muslims equip themselves with a strong belief and righteousness in all their affairs, and also with scientific knowledge and the most sophisticated technology.

In short, Fethullah Gulen's movement is just one more manifestation of what the Muslim Brotherhood has called civilization jihad, albeit a particularly sinister one with its large footprint, penetration of our educational system and well-established, sophisticated and successful influence operations. With this new monograph – the [eighth] in the Center for Security Policy's *Civilization Jihad Readers Series*, we hope to sound an alarm about this multi-faceted and dangerous Islamic supremacist cult that – despite significant setbacks in its native Turkey – constitutes a true Trojan Horse in our midst.

It must be noted that those setbacks are being dealt the Gulen cult and its empire by a rival Islamic supremacist movement: the AK Party and government of Turkish President Recep Tayyep Erdogan. Like erstwhile allies in organized criminal racketeering, these two Islamist mafia dons have had a toxic falling-out after they jointly took down the Ataturk legacy of secular governance in Turkey. Welcome as the rolling up of the Gulen empire and the extradition of its cult leader from the United States would be, nothing in this monograph should be seen as an endorsement of the no-less problematic Erdogan regime's civilization jihadism and its ambitions to restore the Caliphate.

Nearly three years after the successful campaign to prevent a Gulen charter school from setting up in Virginia's Loudoun County, we hope that this monograph will provide the evidence needed to encourage and enable a nation-wide awakening about the subversive nature of the Gulen Movement – and an impetus to the corrective action required to thwart its civilization jihad in America.

Frank J. Gaffney, Jr.
President, Center for Security Policy
10 December 2015

Introduction

Fethullah Gulen is a Turkish Islamic scholar of the thoroughly jihadist Sufi Ottoman tradition with a controversial history and many followers and admirers in both the Islamic and Western worlds. He is known as the spiritual leader of an Islamic socio-political movement that now spans the globe with a network of some 1,500 schools, including universities, in more than 120 countries including the United States (U.S.)

A close analysis, however, must acknowledge some disturbing realities about the ideology that animates Gulen's 50-plus-year old *Hizmet* ('Service') movement. For one thing, not only does Gulen's messaging about Islam track closely with that of the openly jihadist Muslim Brotherhood, but IkhwanWeb ('The Muslim Brotherhood's Official English web site') carries multiple articles that present him in a favorable light.[1] Other—perhaps tenuous—Brotherhood linkages with the Gulen Movement (GM) exist, but for the most part are carefully obscured by the tightly-controlled GM public relations arm. At least as troubling, though, is the unavoidable conclusion that Gulen and his *Hizmet* movement bear much of the responsibility for the destruction of Turkey's secular modernization program and its setback onto a pre-Ataturk, Islamic, even jihadist, neo-Ottoman course.

If Fethullah Gulen's influence were limited to Turkey, a U.S. NATO ally, it would be bad enough. But his educational program, extensive organizational network, and aggressively-pursued influence efforts among educators and legislators, are expanding in the U.S. now, too. Gulen left Turkey in 1998 to avoid prosecution after clashing with the forces of secular democracy then dominating the country. Somehow, he was permitted to emigrate to the U.S. and move into a fortified compound in the Pennsylvania Pocono Mountains, where he has lived in self-imposed exile ever since. Gulen was granted Permanent Legal Resident status in 2008 (making him eligible for citizenship as of this writing). From his Poconos compound, he directs a sprawling international movement that may include as many as several million followers and hundreds of institutions 'inspired' by him whose collective net worth is estimated to

---

[1] *IkhwanWeb*, The Muslim Brotherhood's official English website. Last updated 11-4-2015 at 11:16 AM GMT. Available at http://www.ikhwanweb.com/search.php?srchword=fethullah+gulen

range from \$20-50 billion.[2]   It is Gulen's Turkish-based—but now global—business empire that provides the financial muscle behind the Gulen Movement's power.

Modeled after Gulen's original Turkish schools, the expanding network of Gulenist charter schools now springing up across the U.S. gives pause and well-founded reason for concern among educators, parents and, increasingly, legislators and the policy community. Despite the Gulen charters' reputation as strong STEM (Science, Technology, Engineering, and Math) curriculum schools, because of its secretive *Hizmet* connection, some questionable financial and visa practices, claims from former members of a cult-like structure, a highly segregated role for women, and a lavishly-funded travel program to Turkey for selected officials from academia, government, media, and law enforcement, the Gulen organization in the U.S. finally is attracting some long-overdue scrutiny.

This monograph, "Fethullah Gulen and the Gulenist Movement," offers readers a comprehensive overview of the reclusive figure at the center of this disturbing global enterprise, his philosophy, role in Turkish society, place in the American educational system, and what that growing influence portends for U.S. students and society.

---

2 Berlinski, Claire, "Who is Fethullah Gulen?" City Journal, Autumn 2012. Available at http://www.city-journal.org/2012/22_4_fethullah-gulen.html

The Gulen Movement: Origins, Structure, and Ideology

On 28 August 2015, the *Wall Street Journal* published an opinion piece on Islamic "extremism" written by Fethullah Gulen. That piece, entitled *Muslims Must Combat the Extremist Cancer,*[3] seemed at first glance to include all the right clichés that make Westerners feel better about the threat from jihad. A closer look unfortunately reveals another agenda behind Gulen's soothing words: a whitewashing of Islam on the pretext that it is only "violent radicals" that give the faith a bad image.

Gulen's selective citing of Qur'an verse 5:32 is a good example, as he neglects to inform the reader that this verse was lifted directly out of a pre-existing Jewish text (the 'Oral Torah,' or Mishnah, IV Division 5), is addressed explicitly to "The Children of Israel," and is followed in verse 5:33 by a list of the gruesome punishments which are stipulated by Islam for those who "spread mischief in the land" (i.e., transgress or fail to embrace Islam—like the Jews).[4]

Gulen's own formative influences derive from the Nurcu movement in Turkey. Sheikh Sa'id-i Kurdi (aka Sa'id-i Nursi, 1878–1960) was a Sunni Muslim in the Sufi tradition, whose 'reading circles' crystalized into a resistance movement against Kemal Ataturk's modernization process but yet nevertheless viewed itself as nationalistic and forward-looking. Nursi demanded that the new post-WW I Turkish republic be based on Islamic principles and ruled by Islamic Law (shariah). Gulen was his student and follower. Disdainful of simply proselytizing, though, Gulen instead urges his followers (variously referred to as *Hizmet*, the Fethullah Gulen Community aka FCG, or simply the "Community", Fethullah Gulen's missionaries, the *Nurchilar* religious movement, or *cemaat*) to practice *temsil*—living an Islamic way of life at all times.[5] A televised 1999 speech to his followers, however, shows striking similarity to Muslim Brotherhood messaging and demonstrates how Gulen perceived his movement and the societal transformation he actually sought to achieve in Turkey:

> You must move in the arteries of the system without anyone noticing your existence until you reach all the power centers.... Until the

[3] Gulen, Fethullah, "Muslims Must Combat the Extremist Cancer," *Wall Street Journal*, August 27, 2015. Available at http://www.wsj.com/articles/muslims-must-combat-the-extremist-cancer-1440718377
[4] Spencer, Robert, "The Chapter Fueling ISIS' Genocide? Robert Spencer's Blogging the Qur'an: Sura 5, 'The Table,' *PJ Media*, April 27, 2015. Available at http://pjmedia.com/blog/the-chapter-fueling-isis-genocide-robert-spencers-blogging-the-quran-sura-5-the-table/
[5] Berlinski

conditions are ripe, they [the followers] must continue like this. If they do something prematurely, the world will crush our heads, and Muslims will suffer everywhere, like in the tragedies in Algeria, like in 1982 [in] Syria, . . . like in the yearly disasters and tragedies in Egypt.... The time is not yet right. You must wait for the time when you are complete and conditions are ripe, until we can shoulder the entire world and carry it.... You must wait until such time as you have gotten all the state power, until you have brought to your side all the power of the constitutional institutions in Turkey... Now, I have expressed my feelings and thoughts to you all—in confidence... trusting your loyalty and secrecy. I know that when you leave here, [just] as you discard your empty juice boxes, you must discard the thoughts and the feelings that I expressed here.[6]

A glimpse into the otherwise opaque organizational structure of the global Gulen Movement (GM) was made available through a WikiLeaks publication of a Stratfor analysis of the movement. On 27 February 2012, WikiLeaks began publishing *The Global Intelligence Files*, which comprise over 5 million emails from Stratfor, the Texas-headquartered geo-political intelligence firm. Dated between July 2004 and December 2011, the cache includes an extensive analysis of the GM, dated 18 November 2009 and entitled 'Gulen Movement: Turkey's third power.'[7]

Stratfor's analysis of the GM's organizational structure divides the movement into 3 concentric and overlapping circles:

- Sympathizers make up the outermost circle. It consists of people who attend weekly discussion sessions held in homes and those who receive Gulenist services and charity benefits, students in particular.

- Members make up the middle circle. These include businessmen and others who donate to movement. They support the outer circle sympathizers' activities and pay the salaries of the inner circle.

[6] Sharon-Krespin, Rachel, "Fethullah Gulen's Grand Ambition: Turkey's Islamist Danger," *Middle East Quarterly*, Winter 2009, pp. 55-66. Available at http://www.meforum.org/2045/fethullah-gulens-grand-ambition
[7] 'The Global Intelligence Files," WikiLeaks. Available at http://wl.wikileaks-press.org/gifiles/docs/1532300_gulen-movement-turkey-s-third-power-.html

- Workers make up the inner circle. These include teachers in particular, but also journalists, lobbyists, scholars at think tanks, staff at business groups, and others. The workers are mostly committed members of the movement as well as some former students. They are sometimes called *Altin Nesil* (Golden Generation) and can be considered Gulenist disciples.

The three groups interact extensively: Gulenist businesses advertise heavily on Gulenist media. Gulenist media run stories on Gulenist sympathizers, members, workers, businesses, and schools. Gulenist members and sympathizers take holidays in Gulenist-owned hotels, shop at Gulenist-owned stores, and invest with Gulenist banks and finance companies. Graduates of Gulenist schools funded by Gulenist businesses and members often end up becoming teachers at Gulenist schools overseas. And, of course, Gulenist media, funded by Gulenist businesses and members, react sharply to any criticism of Gulen himself.[8]

---

[8] The Global Intelligence Files

Moving in the Arteries of the System—Then a Rupture

Described as a "charismatic imam"[9], Gulen has a long political history in Turkey but has also been identified as the leader of a "shadowy Islamist sect."[10] Over the decades since the founding of *Hizmet* in the 1960s, Gulen successfully built two extensive networks: one was the international educational network of schools and the other an extensive network of Gulenist cadres within the Turkish judiciary and police. Their collective influence worked inexorably to corrode Turkey's modernizing social reforms of the early 20th century from within even as the internal struggle for stability led the military to intervene four times (1960, 1971, 1980, 1997) to restore order and preserve Ataturk's secular legacy. Although already in the U.S. at the time, Gulen was tried in absentia in Turkey in 2000 on charges that he was trying to replace Turkey's secular government with an Islamic one. Finally acquitted in 2008, Gulen nevertheless obviously was aiming to do exactly that.

Until Gulen's explosive 2013 split with his former ally, then-Prime Minister Recep Tayyip Erdogan, he had a broad following in Turkey's ruling Justice and Development Party (the AKP), as well as within the ranks of the police and judicial system, and had managed to infiltrate much of the state bureaucracy also. In fact, up to that point, it seemed that Gulen and Erdogan were moving in ideological tandem, given the strongly anti-secular, pro-shariah, and Islamic philosophy of governance they shared. Indeed, Gulen's support has been called 'vital' to Erdogan's successful consolidation of state power while Gulenists among the national police force were instrumental in the brutal suppression of the June 2013 demonstrations in Taksim Square.[11]

The catalyst for the eventual rupture, therefore, may best be described as rivalry for power between two ambitious men. The AKP/Erdogan accusations of establishing a "parallel state" erupted in late 2013, just as Erdogan was transitioning

---

[9] Beauchamp, Scott, "120 American Charter Schools and One Secretive Turkish Cleric," The Atlantic, August 12, 2014. Available at http://www.theatlantic.com/education/archive/2014/08/120-american-charter-schools-and-one-secretive-turkish-cleric/375923/

[10] Sharon-Krespin, Rachel, "Fethullah Gulen's Grand Ambition: Turkey's Islamist Danger," The Middle East Quarterly, Winter 2009, pp. 55-66. Available at http://www.meforum.org/2045/fethullah-gulens-grand-ambition

[11] Birnbaum, Michael, "In Turkey protests, splits in Erdogan's base," Washington Post, June 14, 2013. Available at https://www.washingtonpost.com/world/erdogan-offers-concessions-to-turkeys-protesters/2013/06/14/9a87fff6-d4bf-11e2-a73e-826d299ff459_story.html

into the presidency following eleven years as an increasingly authoritarian Prime Minister; his move against Gulen was in fact a somewhat delayed response to what can be seen as a triggering Gulen move, a two-year *Hizmet* corruption investigation of figures with government links. Looking back, it is now evident that from about 2010 onward, Erdogan and his AKP party already had begun to consolidate their power by taking on the military power centers that had acted as guardians of the Kemal Ataturk Republic for nearly a century. Over the period, hundreds of senior Turkish officers were jailed or forced into early retirement, eviscerating the military's capabilities to intervene in the government but also deeply affecting its operational effectiveness as well.[12] By the time of the 2013-14 break between Erdogan and Gulen, the president was in a strong position to challenge Gulen for dominance as well, and thousands of *Hizmet* supporters in the ranks of the Turkish police and judiciary were dismissed or reassigned as he cracked down and further consolidated his own support.

The Gulenist Movement itself was declared a terrorist organization by the AKP in 2014, which labeled it the Gülenist Terror Organization (FETÖ), and Gulen was named to Turkey's most-wanted list. An arrest warrant in absentia was issued in Turkey on 19 December 2014 and a second arrest warrant plus an Interpol red notice went out on 24 February 2015.[13] Yet another arrest warrant in absentia for Gulen was issued on 9 November 2015. The U.S. and Turkey are signatories to a mutual extradition treaty, but legal experts say the crime in question must be recognized by both countries and it seems unlikely that the U.S. government will honor Turkey's extradition request for Gulen. In late October 2015, Reuters reported that the government of Turkey had hired the international law firm, Amsterdam and Partners LLP (with offices in both London and Washington, D.C.) to investigate the worldwide activities of the Gulen Movement. Speaking on 26 October, 2015 at the National Press Club in Washington, D.C., founding partner Robert Amsterdam cited "penetration of the Turkish judiciary and police, as well as its political lobbying abroad"[14] among the concerns that brought his law firm into the widening campaign against the GM by the Turkish government.

---

[12] Jones, Dorian, "Legacy of Coup Probes Haunt Effectiveness of Turkish Military," *VOA News*, July 08, 2015. Available at http://www.voanews.com/content/legacy-of-coup-probes-haunt-effectiveness-of-turkish-military/2853540.html

[13] "Arrest Warrant in Absentia, Red Notice Issued for Gulen," available at http://m.ulkucumedya.com/arrest-warrant-in-absentia-red-notice-issued-for-gulen-23098h.htm

[14] "Republic of Turkey Retains Amsterdam & Partners LLP on Expanding Gulen Investigation into Africa and U.S. Charter Schools," Reuters, 26 October 2015. Available at

Official Concerns about the Gulenist Agenda

Some senior U.S. officials have readily accepted Gulen's carefully-cultivated self-image as the face of 'moderate Islam.' Then-NY Senator Hillary Clinton spoke at a 2007 'Friendship Dinner' organized by the Gulenist Turkish Cultural Center.[15] Former Secretary of State Madeleine Albright spoke at a 2008 Gulen Institute Luncheon Forum and attended a Houston, TX Gulen Turquoise Center ribbon-cutting ceremony the same year. Graham Fuller, a former CIA officer and the author of several books on Islam, said (admiringly) that Gülen is leading "one of the most important movements in the Muslim world today." [16] Others are not so easily convinced, however; speaking to the *New York Times* in 2012, one senior U.S. official (who requested anonymity to avoid breaching diplomatic protocol), said that "We are troubled by the secretive nature of the Gulen movement, all the smoke and mirrors. It is clear they want influence and power. We are concerned there is a hidden agenda to challenge secular Turkey and guide the country in a more Islamic direction."[17]

U.S. diplomatic officials posted to the Embassy in Ankara and consulates throughout the country were well aware of Fethullah Gulen, his movement, and their impact on the AKP-secularist struggle within Turkish society. From 2003-2013, according to media accounts detailing State Department reporting regarding the Gulen Movement, the number of official cables increased significantly. Concerns most often expressed included the institutionalization of the Gulen Movement worldwide through its network of schools, the infiltration of government organizations, the sincerity of Gulen narratives about interfaith dialogue, its vast network of business associations, and Gulen ownership of multiple media outlets.[18]

In 2005, the U.S. Embassy in Ankara reportedly discussed a decision by U.S. immigration authorities that, for the first time, denied Gulen the right to travel

---

http://www.reuters.com/article/2015/10/26/amsterdampartners-idUSnPn8rXT59+8c+PRN20151026#QmqypXuVPi0Lhp5q.97

[15] 'Hillary Clinton Participated Friendship Dinner in NY," *YouTube*, uploaded Sep 20, 2007. Available at https://www.youtube.com/watch?v=8xnLTYGWo-o

[16] Hansen, Suzy, "The Global Imam," *The New Republic*, November 10, 2010. Available at http://www.newrepublic.com/article/world/magazine/79062/global-turkey-imam-fethullah-gulen

[17] Bilefsky, Dan and Sebnem Arsu, "Turkey Feels Sway of Reclusive Cleric in the U.S.," *New York Times*, April 24, 2012. Available at http://www.nytimes.com/2012/04/25/world/middleeast/turkey-feels-sway-of-fethullah-gulen-a-reclusive-cleric.html?_r=0

[18] ÖZGE ÖZÇELIK, "A decade of the Gülen Movement on WikiLeaks: More than meets the eye," Daily Sabah, August 10, 2015. Available at http://www.dailysabah.com/features/2015/08/11/a-decade-of-the-gulen-movement-on-wikileaks-more-than-meets-the-eye

outside of the U.S., where he'd lived since 1998. According to sources familiar with the relevant cable from Stuart Smith, the U.S. vice consul general of the Intelligence Department in Ankara, three ranking members of the National Police (reportedly then-deeply penetrated by Gulenist loyalists) sought a meeting with U.S. diplomats in Istanbul for the purpose of requesting whether the "FBI could provide some sort of clean bill of health" for Fethullah Gülen.[19]

In one 2009 cable sent from the U.S. Embassy in Ankara, the mission described the extent of the Gulen business empire that included schools, the Journalists and Writers Foundation, various businesses, and several media outlets, including 'Zaman,' 'Today's Zaman' (English language), 'Samanyolu TV,' and 'Aksiyon Weekly.' Acknowledging the Movement's stated goals of interfaith dialogue and tolerance, the Embassy report yet pointed to concern among some Turks that Gulen "has a deeper and possibly insidious political agenda." That concern reportedly was especially pronounced among the ranks of the Turkish military that were all-too-aware of Gulenist newspapers like 'Zaman' that consistently attacked their role as defenders of the Ataturk legacy, in order (as they saw it) to undermine the military and transform Turkey into an Islamic republic.[20]

An April 2011 article by the *Philadelphia Inquirer* reported in some detail about concerns among U.S. consular officials working in Turkey that a large number of Turkish men were applying for visas to work at U.S. charter schools associated with followers of Fethullah Gulen. Citing a classified cable from 2006 that was released by WikiLeaks as well as an independent analysis of its own, the *Inquirer* noted that the number of H-1B visas had grown substantially in the period 2006-2011. A second issue, as reported by the *Inquirer,* involves federal investigations into allegations that U.S. Gulenist charter school employees were being required to kick back part of their salaries to the *Hizmet.*[21] These and other concerns about the GM will be addressed in greater detail below.

---

[19] ÖZÇELIK
[20] ÖZÇELIK
[21] Woodall, Martha and Claudio Gatti, "WikiLeaks Files detail U.S. unease over Turks and charter schools," Philadelphia *Inquirer*, April 04, 2011. Available at http://articles.philly.com/2011-04-04/news/29380536_1_charter-schools-fethullah-gulen-truebright-science-academy

Der Spiegel Accusations

The respected German weekly '*Der Spiegel*' also raised serious questions about Fethullah Gulen and his worldwide movement in a pair of highly critical articles published in 2012 and 2014. The magazine cites individuals who broke ties with Gulen and who characterize *Hizmet* as an 'ultraconservative secret society' and Gulen himself as an ideologue who tolerates no dissent,' is 'only interested in power and influence,' and 'dreams of a new age in which Islam will dominate the West.'[22]

According to *Der Spiegel*, these critics say that the Gulen Movement, or religious community ('*cemaat*' in Turkish), 'educates its future leaders throughout the world in so-called 'houses of light,' which they describe as a kind of combined shared student residence and school for studying Islam where a rigid daily routine of work, prayer, and (very little) sleep is overseen by a supervisor who guards the students as in a prison. Indeed, Gulen wrote in his book '*Fasildan Fasila*' ('From Time to Time') that students should sleep but three hours a day, use two hours for other needs, and 'must devote the rest entirely to *Hizmet*.'[23]

The Gulen Movement's finances are especially murky, according to *Der Spiegel*: while wealthy donors contribute millions to the movement, '*Fethullacis*' (as Gulen followers are called) donate an average of ten percent of their income to the group, with some giving as much as 70 percent (willingly or unwillingly is not always clear). And yet, the Movement has no headquarters, no address, is not registered anywhere, and has no central bank account.[24]

In its 2014 article, "The Preacher Who Could Topple Erdogan," *Der Spiegel* describes the Erdogan-Gulen split, which, at the time, seemed to threaten the very standing of Erdogan's Justice and Development Party (AKP) in Turkish society. Subsequent events, culminating in a November 2015 parliamentary victory for the AKP, later dispelled such concerns (at least for the time being) while solidifying Erdogan's increasingly dictatorial grip on power in Turkey. That drive to unchallenged control clearly led to the falling out between the former jihadist allies, with Erdogan accusing the *Fethullacis* of creating 'a state within a state.'[25]

---

[22] Popp, Maximilian, "The Shadowy World of the Islamic Gulen Movement," Der Spiegel, 08/08/2012. Available online at http://www.spiegel.de/international/germany/guelen-movement-accused-of-being-a-sect-a-848763-druck.html

[23] *Ibid*

[24] Ibid

[25] Popp, Maximilian, "A Brother's Vengeance: The Preacher Who Could Topple Erdogan," Der Spiegel, 1/09/2014. Available at http://www.spiegel.de/international/world/turkey-erdogan-sees-power-threatened-by-muslim-cleric-guelen-a-942296-druck.html

The Gulen Movement in the U.S.

The Charter Schools

Despite the sprawling size of the Gulen Movement (GM) worldwide, the vast number of its academic, business, and cultural affiliates, and even after the widely-covered 2013 fracture of the Erdogan-Gulen partnership in Turkey, Fethullah Gulen and his movement remain largely unknown and even less understood in the U.S. As one of the best-organized Islamic grass-roots organizations in the world, the GM merits a much closer look, particularly as its influence—and charter school network—are expanding throughout the country.

After the fall of the Soviet Union, Gulen's followers established hundreds of schools in the newly independent Central Asian countries, attempting to rekindle a Turkish cultural kinship there. Around the world, there are more than a dozen universities affiliated with the Gulen Movement, including three in the U.S. (See Appendix B for a list of these universities.) Virginia International University[26] is located in Fairfax, Virginia, American Islamic College[27] in Chicago, Illinois, and North American University[28] in Houston, Texas. None displays any hint of a Gulen Movement connection at its website, but the American Islamic College's Board of Trustees[29] alone should set alarm bells ringing. Among the listed Board members is one Dr. Abdullah Omar Naseef, a Saudi closely-connected not only to the royal family but to both al-Qa'eda and the Muslim Brotherhood as well. He was, in fact, a top al-Qa'eda financier prior to 9/11 as founder of the Rabita Trust, a formally designated foreign terrorist organization under American law. Naseef also founded the *Institute of Muslim Minority Affairs* and served on its journal's editorial board for a period of at least seven years (1996-2003) together with Huma Abedin, who was working through the period at the White House and elsewhere in various capacities for Hillary Clinton.[30]

The Gulen Movement also is closely affiliated with the University of Houston, where the Gulen Institute, which bills itself as a 'non-profit research organization dedicated to the `promotion of peace and civic welfare,' is a joint

---

[26] Virginia International University, http://viu.edu/
27 American Islamic College, , http://www.aicusa.edu
28 North American University, http://www.na.edu/
29 American Islamic College, http://www.aicusa.edu/about-aic/trustees-2/
30 McCarthy, Andrew, "The Huma Unmentionables," National Review Online, July 24, 2013. Available at http://www.nationalreview.com/corner/354351/huma-unmentionables-andrew-c-mccarthy

initiative of the Graduate College of Social Work and the Institute of Interfaith Dialogue (now known as Dialogue Institute of the Southwest). According to its website, the Gulen Institute 'offers research grants and scholarships, organizes lecture series at the University of Houston, and facilitates workshops and panel discussions…' and also offers 'cultural exchange trips to graduate students at the University of Houston…'[31] More on the Dialogue Institute of the Southwest follows under the *GM Cultural Centers: The Raindrop Turkish House* section below.

Here in the U.S., it is the Gulen K-12 charter schools that draw the most attention and concern. Since the first Gulen school in the U.S. opened in 1999, the network as grown to some 150 Gulenist schools with over 60,000 students enrolled in the U.S. (See Appendix A for a list of GM charter schools in the U.S.) Board members of these charter schools are primarily Turkish or Turkic (as are the overwhelmingly foreign-born male teachers and school administrators) and often have ties to other Gulenist organizations.

GM schools are funded in part by private donations from the far-flung movement's supporters but, as charters in the U.S., are also taxpayer-subsidized. Gulen schools typically emphasize a strong STEM (Science, Technology, Engineering, and Math) curriculum,[32] which usually yields high test scores and students who excel academically. This is the part parents tend to love, but it's the more subtle messaging that increasingly is giving rise to concern (along with persistent financial and legal irregularities, explored in more detail below). There is no evidence that Gulen charter schools in the U.S. include Islamic indoctrination in their curriculum, and yet, as the account below reveals, there clearly is at a minimum, a pro-Turkish agenda that infuses the program. For instance, GM charter schools usually include Turkish language classes, which may be mandatory in some grade levels, an overt emphasis on Turkish culture, and student participation in Turkish Language Olympics.

---

[31] The Gulen Institute, http://www.guleninstitute.org/
32 Higgins, Sharon, "Largest charter network in U.S.: Schools tied to Turkey," Washington Post, March 27, 2012. Available at https://www.washingtonpost.com/blogs/answer-sheet/post/largest-charter-network-in-us-schools-tied-to-turkey/2012/03/23/gIQAoaFzcS_blog.html

The GM schools' Turkish agenda was inadvertently exposed when a 2009 GM Turkish-language website (*'Sabah'*) revealed a disturbing conversation among the writer, Nazli Ilicak, and other GM colleagues.[33]

> We discussed the subject among ourselves: If 600 schools are bought this way in the United States – and that's what the members of the Gulen movement are striving to do, - and if 200 students graduate from each one of these schools, then 120 thousand sympathizers of Turkey join the mainstream out there every year. We are trying to lobby against the Armenian genocide resolution every year. And yet, through education, we can teach tens of thousands of people the Turkish language and our national anthem, introduce them to our culture and WIN them over. And this is what the Gulen movement is striving for.

Tellingly, once the GM realized the conversation had been translated into English and made public in the U.S., it disappeared from the original website. Likewise, when GM school officials are questioned about their school's connections to the GM, the responses are often either ambiguous or flat denials. The argument filed with the Department of Homeland Security (DHS) on Gulen's behalf when he was appealing a DHS ruling that he did not meet the criteria to qualify as an "alien of extraordinary ability" for purposes of immigration to the U.S., however, offers the most compelling evidence of precisely such connections. According to the *Philadelphia Inquirer*, Gulen's successful appeal, that won him a green card from a federal judge in 2008, emphasized his renown as an educational figure.[34] The *Washington Post* went even further, writing that Gulen's lawyers had openly "identified him as 'head of the Gulen Movement,' and an important educational figure who had 'overseen' the creation of a network of schools in the U.S. and around the world."[35]

---

[33] Steller, Tim, "Sr. Reporter: How Gulen schools create Turkey sympathizers—a columnist's view," May 28, 2010. Available at http://tucson.com/news/blogs/senor-reporter/article_41e34294-6aae-11df-93fe-001cc4c03286.html For the original Turkish language text, see
http://www.sabah.com.tr/yazarlar/ilicak/2009/09/02/gulenin_kulaklarini_cinlattik
34 Woodall and Gatti
35 Strauss, Valerie, "Islamic cleric linked to U.S. charters schools involved in Turkey's political drama," Washington Post, December 23, 2013. Available at https://www.washingtonpost.com/news/answer-sheet/wp/2013/12/26/islamic-cleric-linked-to-u-s-charter-schools-involved-in-turkeys-political-drama/

All of which apparently deliberate ambiguity contributes to the network's secretive image and growing concern among educators, law enforcement, and parents that such schools may function to some extent as a feeder system to the GM itself.

Even a devote as sympathetic to Fethullah Gulen as Hakan Yavuz, assistant professor at the University of Utah's Middle East Center, and the co-author (together with Georgetown's John Esposito) of a laudatory book on the GM, "Turkish Islam and the Secular State: the Gulen Movement,"[36] was honest enough to tell the *New York Times* the truth about the GM's Islamic agenda. According to the *Times*, Yavuz said

> ...that he sees the [Gulen] schools as "the foundation for the movement's attempts to grow in the United States. The main purpose right now is to show the positive side of Islam and to make Americans sympathize with Islam."[37]

The extent to which the multi-faceted GM is organized within the U.S. similarly is not well-understood, but reporting that has emerged suggests a far more structured administrative apparatus than generally realized. For example, in 2012, a Turkish teacher who formerly taught at a U.S. Gulen school told the FBI that the Movement 'had divided the U.S. into five regions, with a general manager in each who coordinates the activities of the schools, and related foundations and cultural centers.'[38]

Additionally, Gulen charter schools regularly sponsor trips to Turkey for students. GM-associated organizations, not all of which openly identify themselves as connected to the Gulen Movement,[39] but rather present as Turkish 'cultural' groups, have also provided thousands of all-expenses-paid trips to Turkey for academics, journalists, politicians and other public officials. Sightseeing is a big part of such 'cultural immersion' trips, but so are visits to GM-affiliated institutions.[40] A partial list of Gulen-affiliated cultural organizations in the U.S. can be found in Appendix E

---

[36] Book available at http://www.amazon.com/Turkish-Islam-Secular-State-Contemporary/dp/0815630409
[37] Saul, Stephanie, "Charter Schools Tied to Turkey Grow in Texas," New York Times, June 6, 2011. Available at http://www.nytimes.com/2011/06/07/education/07charter.html
[38] Ahlert, Arnold, "Stealth Islamic Charter Schools Under Investigation," Front Page Magazine, October 31, 2012. Available at http://www.frontpagemag.com/fpm/163505/stealth-islamist-charter-schools-under-arnold-ahlert
[39] See this representative list for some of the thousands of U.S. and international Gulen Movement-linked organizations: http://www.gulenmovement.us/links
[40] Higgins

below. Even more disturbing, allegations about fraudulent funding practices by Gulenist groups for trips to Turkey by members of the U.S. Congress surfaced in 2015 and will be addressed below.

Allegations and Investigations

All-Expense-Paid 'Cultural' Excursions—or Influence Operations?

Although GM leadership denies that there is any top-down organized attempt to seek political influence through donations to political campaigns in the U.S. or the hundreds of all-expense-paid trips to Turkey that have been provided to key members of local, state, and federal legislatures, evidence of such involvement has been mounting. For example, campaign donations from people connected to Gulen schools to Texas Congressional Representative Sheila Jackson Lee totaled $23,000 in October 2013, which was a considerable sum, given that, according to documents filed with the Federal Election Commission, she raised a total of $130,000 that particular election cycle. Other liberal Democrats, including Yvette Clarke and Al Green, and conservative Republicans like Ted Poe and Pete Olson, have all benefitted from donors affiliated with Gülen in one way or another. [41] In response, GM representatives point out that the Movement is a nonprofit, non-governmental organization that does not endorse candidates or engage in political fundraising for any candidates.

Concerns about the GM, including a look at its U.S. network of charter schools, were aired on a *60 Minutes* piece with reporter Leslie Stahl in May 2012. [42] *Turkish Invitations*, the GM watchdog group, has compiled a long list[43] of accounts about trips to Turkey sponsored and paid for by a host of various Gulen affiliates, including the Atlas Foundation of Louisiana, [44] the Raindrop Foundation, several different U.S. branches of the Dialogue Foundation, the Niagara Foundation, [45] the North Carolina-based Divan Center, [46] the Pacifica Institute[47], and others. Those targeted for such junkets included civic leaders, Christian and Jewish faith community

---

[41] Gray, Rosie, "Secretive Turkish Movement Buys U.S. Influence." Buzz Feed News, July 23, 2014. Available at http://www.buzzfeed.com/rosiegray/secretive-turkish-movement-buys-us-influence#.ioeQW04NB

42 "U.S. Charter Schools Tied to Powerful Turkish Imam," CBS News, May 13, 2012. Program script available at http://www.cbsnews.com/news/us-charter-schools-tied-to-powerful-turkish-imam/ Segment available on YouTube at https://www.youtube.com/watch?v=ktl--IDnM7I

43 "Accounts of Gulenist Turkey trips," available here: http://turkishinvitations.weebly.com/gulenist-turkey-trip-accounts.html

44 Atlas Foundation, http://atlaslouisiana.org/

45 Niagara Foundation, https://www.niagarafoundation.org/niagara/fethullah-gulen/

46 Divan Center, http://www.divancenter.org/

47 Pacifica Institute, http://pacificainstitute.org/

leaders, journalists, state legislators, students, and university presidents, professors, and trustees.[48] Typically, according to recorded trip accounts, those invited know that it is the GM that sponsors them, but seem often to be carefully selected for their lack of familiarity about Fethullah Gulen or his agenda related to Islam and Turkey.

The Gulenists do not always reveal their sponsorship of all-expense-paid trips to Turkey, however. In the case of hundreds of trips for members of the U.S. Congress, GM funding was in fact carefully concealed. A *USA Today* investigation reported on 29 October 2015[49] that the GM secretly and illegally funded "as many as 200 trips to Turkey" for members of Congress since 2008. According to investigators, the House Ethics Committee approved all of the trips based on allegedly falsified disclosure forms that disguised the Gulenist identities of groups that presented themselves as non-profit organizations.[50]

Turkish-Gulen Charter Schools Under a Cloud

Numerous Gulen Movement-affiliated charter schools across the U.S. are the subject of controversy, scandal and investigation by local school board as well as federal authorities. Below will be found a representative listing of some of these which have emerged into public view by way of the media. While neither conclusive nor exhaustive, the list and the cases it represents indicate, at a minimum, that there are serious issues with the GM charter school network in the U.S. that are giving rise to justifiable concern among parents, students, and authorities at local, regional, and federal levels.

The FBI and the Department of Labor and Education have begun investigating at least two practices of concern involving the Gulen schools nationwide: their extraordinarily high and disproportionate utilization of H-1B visas to import teachers and other personnel from Turkey to staff their charter schools, and the reportedly higher pay for Turkish staffers who are then compelled to return a portion of their salaries to *Hizmet* (that is, to the Gulen Movement). Foreign-trained teachers and other workers are eligible for employment in the U.S. via the H-1B non-

---

[48] Turkish Invitations, http://turkishinvitations.weebly.com/gulenist-turkey-trip-accounts.html
49 Singer, Paul and Paulina Firozi, "Turkish faith movement secretly funded 200 trips for lawmakers and staff," USA Today, October 29, 2015. Available at
http://www.usatoday.com/story/news/politics/2015/10/29/turkish-faith-movement-secretly-funded-200-trips-lawmakers-and-staff/74535104/
50 USA Today

immigrant work visa which is good for 3 years, renewable for one additional 3 year term, or the shorter 1 year J-1 exchange visa, which is renewable for an additional 2 year term. The J-1 visa is intended to promote cultural exchange. The H-1B visa allows hiring foreign workers in a "specialty occupation that requires theoretical and practical application of a body of highly specialized knowledge, along with at least a bachelor's degree or its equivalent in the specialization".[51] Even though there is an annual cap on the number of H-1B visas that can be issued, primary and secondary schools in some instances can circumvent the cap. Federal law has exempted institutions of higher education, nonprofit and government research institutions, and institutions related to or affiliated with them, from the visa cap. For example, a Texas school district was able to access this exemption by having its bilingual teachers hired through a university certification program, which included a 2 month public school internship.

The typical claim made by school districts and/or charter schools utilizing the H-1B visas for foreign recruitment of teachers and other school personnel, is the "shortage" of qualified American workers. But "the H-1B program demands no test of the labor market by employers (to see if American workers are available for these jobs)…" and as Center for Immigration Studies fellow David North notes, operates to "deprive American teachers of jobs".[52]

Abundant documentation and first-hand testimony exist to support the allegations that the Gulen-affiliated network of schools is the largest consumer of H-1B visas for school staffing in the U.S. Indeed, it has been reported that these schools exceed the application rate for these visas of even the largest urban school districts.

Based on the list of "Top 100 H-1b Visa Sponsors In Secondary School Education Since 2008",[53] published at myvisajobs.com, the following analysis was drawn by a Gulen Charter School watchdog group:[54]

- The Gulen schools and their related organizations account for 31.5% of all H-1B visa applications requested by the top 100 secondary school education H1B visa sponsors

---

[51] See U.S. Department of Labor, H-1B Program at http://www.dol.gov/whd/immigration/h1b.htm
52 North, David, "Primer for Reporters Looking into the H-1B Program," Center for Immigration Studies, July 1, 2015. Available at http://cis.org/miano/primer-reporters-looking-h-1b-program
53 http://www.myvisajobs.com/Elementary-and-Secondary-Schools-6111-2015IN.htm
54 "Gulen schools and their booming H1B visa applications," July 23, 2010. Available at http://charterschoolscandals.blogspot.com/search?q=H1B+visa+applications

- Of the top 100 secondary school education H-1B visa sponsors, 34 of the 100 sponsors were Gulen schools or their related organizations

- A total of 4,277 secondary school visas were requested by the top 100 sponsors and of these, Gulen schools, or their related organizations, submitted 1,349

- There were fewer than 100 U.S. Gulen schools in operation during those years

- By way of contrast, Global Teachers Research Resources (a teacher headhunting organization), ranked #2 with 325 visa applications. GTRR's newsletters reveal a wide range of teacher nationalities.

- Public school districts also applied for visas. In fact, seven of the top-20 largest school districts in the country were also top-100 sponsors for visa applications. These seven districts represent nearly 2,900,000 students attending approximately 3,831 schools.

- When averaged, seven of the top-20 largest school districts in the country submitted one H-1B visa application for every 6.2 schools.

- The average number of visa applications for the Gulen schools was 13.5 H-1B visa applications per school.

- The Cosmos Foundation, which operates Gulen schools in several states, ranked #1 for H-1B visa applications.

The magnitude of the H-1B visa use by Gulen identified schools was confirmed by a partial study undertaken by CIS fellow David North. Even though his study group only included 86 employers with 10 or more H-1B visa applications granted for K-12 teachers in FY 2010, he found that the 86 employers could hire "10,065 new workers of the national total of 13,157 in this category; in other words, these 86 employers employed 76 percent of the new K-12 H-1Bs granted that year." His study also determined that of the 86 K-12 employers, 13 were Gulen organizations in 12 states and that as compared to the approved number of H-1B visas for Gulen entities in FY2009 (684 in 25 states as reported by the *Philadelphia Inquirer*), his study dealing with only 12 states and 686 approvals in FY2010 reflects that "the Gulen charters were either expanding quite rapidly, or were using a yet larger percentage of foreign workers in them, or both."[55]

Here is a list of close to a dozen representative cases in which U.S. charter schools affiliated with the Gulen Movement have come under scrutiny due to allegations ranging from improper visa and hiring practices and financial mismanagement to discriminatory admissions policies. In fact, as of late October 2015, no fewer than 19 Gulen schools in as many as 7 states were being investigated by the FBI.

1. In 2013, the Lancaster, PA school board rejected a Gulen Charter School application to open the Academy of Business and Entrepreneurship for multiple reasons, including parental misgivings about the proposed curriculum, the withdrawal of letters of support, and apparent 'cut and paste' segments in the application taken from other charter school applications which had no relevance to the application at hand.[56]

2. The Gulenist Concept Schools operate 16 Horizon Science Academies across Ohio. One of these—the Horizon Science Academy Denison, in Cleveland, OH—has been the target of an investigation ongoing since 2008 by the Department of Labor into its use—and possible misuse—of H-1B visas. During the federal probe, auditors also reportedly found some unusual line item entries in the school administrator's books, including fees paid to people living in Turkey and people never employed by the school. There was even an item listed as $13,000 for "illegal immigration fees." The schools' property owner, from whom the schools lease property, lives in Turkey but is being paid a total of $600,000 over a period of 5 years.[57]

---

[55] David North, "Primer for Reporters"

[56] "School District of Lancaster board rejects charter for controversial business school," Lancaster Online, March 2013. This article oddly has been removed from the website of the Lancaster Online but previously was available at http://lancasteronline.com/article/local/828084_School-District-of-Lancaster-board-rejects-charter-for-controversial-business-school.html#ixzz2O6C8wGf0

[57] Regan, Ron, "Exclusive 5 On Your Side investigation uncovers federal probe into Ohio charter schools," Newsnet5, May 16, 2011. Available at http://www.newsnet5.com/news/local-

3. In a similar 2011 investigation over hiring practices, the U.S. Department of Labor looked into the teacher hiring practices of the Gulenist Horizon Science academies throughout the state of Ohio (including three in Columbus and a total of 17 statewide). They are part of a broader network of charter schools called Concept Schools. At issue was the Horizon use of H-1B visas to bring in Turkish national employees.[58] As of 2014 (and perhaps as late as 2015), the investigation was still ongoing.[59]

4. Transparency concerns related to Gulen charter schools are exacerbated by local officials who publicly seek to deny school associations with the GM. An example from the Quest Charter Academy in Peoria, IL arose in 2011, when Peoria Chamber of Commerce executive director Rob Parks told a local media affiliate (WMBD-TV) that there was no link between the GM and the Quest school. The school principal, Engin Karatas (who uses the last name 'Blackstone,' the English language meaning of 'Karatas'), formerly was the principal from 2007-2010 at Horizon Science Academy Toledo Charter School in Toledo, OH. Before that, from 2006-2007, he was Assistant Principal at Horizon Science Academy Denison Middle Charter School in Cleveland, OH. Both schools are managed by Concept Schools, which also manages the Peoria Quest school. All are part of the GM network of U.S. charter schools, as readily confirmed online where a list of the Gulen charter schools in the U.S. may be found.[60]

5. In February 2013, the Loudoun County, VA school board voted to deny a charter school application for the Loudoun County Math and IT Academy, which was to have been modeled after Chesapeake Science Point, a Gulenist school in Anne Arundel, MD.

news/investigations/exclusive-5-on-your-side-investigation-uncovers-federal-probe-into-ohio-charter-schools

58 Smith Richards, Jennifer, "Feds Question Charter Schools' Foreign Teacher Hiring Practices," The Columbus Dispatch, May 20, 2011. Available at http://www.edweek.org/ew/articles/2011/05/20/33mct_ohchartervisas.h30.html

59 Pilcher, James, "Charter schools use Turkish ties, visas to get teachers," Cincinnati Enquirer, October 6, 2014. Available at http://www.cincinnati.com/story/news/2014/10/05/charter-school-turns-turkish-teachers/16791669/

60 "Peoria's Quest Charter School is part of the Gulen Movement from Turkey," Peoria Story, June 18, 2011. Available at http://peoriastory.typepad.com/peoriastory/2011/06/peorias-quest-charter-school-is-part-of-the-gulen-movement-from-turkey.html See also the list of U.S. Gulen schools at http://turkishinvitations.weebly.com/list-of-us-schools.html

Unfortunately for the Loudoun application process, that school reportedly continued to experience problems with its curriculum six-seven years after its establishment. Further, as school officials reviewed the charter school application, they cited a lack of detail in the applicants' instruction, financial and staffing plans. Significant gaps were cited in the academic and operational plans with regard to curriculum, finances, and the transportation plan. [61]

6. A May 2015 affidavit filing with the Cuyahoga County Common Pleas Court in Ohio claimed discriminatory and other possibly illegal practices at the Horizon Science Academy Denison Middle School in Cleveland, OH (noted above for a federal probe of its H-1B visa practices). In this new filing, a former Turkish Muslim employee of the school from 2006-2009, claimed that the Gulen movement, which had brought him to the U.S. from Turkey, demanded cash kickbacks deducted from his pay and pension.[62]

7. In 2012, *The New York Times* exposed three Gulen schools in Fulton County, Georgia for defaulting on bonds and improperly granting hundreds of thousands of dollars in contracts to businesses and groups tied to the Gulen movement. The *NYT* piece also referred to its own earlier reporting in 2011 about a similar case involving 36 Gulenist schools in Texas that had 'granted millions of dollars in construction and renovation contracts to firms run by Turkish-Americans with ties' to the GM. The Fulton Science Academy Middle School in Alpharetta, GA was denied a renewal of its charter in 2012 while a full audit of two other Gulenist schools—the Fulton Science Academy High School and Fulton Sunshine Academy, an elementary school—remained ongoing.[63]

---

[61] Nadler, Danielle, "Loudoun County School board rejects Gulen Charter application," February 27, 2013. Available at http://gulencharterschoolsusa.blogspot.com/2013/02/loudoun-county-school-board-rejects.html

62 Smythe, Julie Carr, "Turkish religious movement influence alleged at Ohio school," WKBN First News, June 15, 2015. Available at http://wkbn.com/2015/06/15/turkish-religious-movement-influence-alleged-at-ohio-school/ See also an interview by Frank Gaffney, President of the Center for Security Policy, with Mary Addi on practices at this and other Gulen schools here: http://www.youtube.com/watch?v=DReAWz1mSZo&feature=player_embedded

63 Saul, Stephanie, "Audits for 3 Georgia Schools Tied to Turkish Movement," The New York Times, June 5, 2012. Available at http://www.nytimes.com/2012/06/06/us/audits-for-3-georgia-charter-schools-tied-to-gulen-movement.html?_r=4&

8. Following a lengthy investigation by the Department of Education's Office for Civil Rights into discriminatory admissions procedures that limited the number of disabled students and those with limited English proficiency on its campuses, it was announced in November 2014 that the Gulenist Harmony Public schools charter network in Texas would modify its admission policies to ensure equal access and opportunity for disabled students and those for whom English was a second language.[64]

9. A months-long audit of the Cosmos Foundation which operates the Harmony network of Gulenist charter schools in Texas concluded in July 2012 that $186,197 in federal grant money intended to improve education for students with disabilities or those from low-income families had been misspent.[65]

10. In April 2010, the Utah State Office of Education decided to shut down the Gulen Movement's financially struggling Beehive Science and Technology Academy. Alleged financial mismanagement reportedly included large sums spent on immigration fees for Turkish teachers with little or no prior teaching experience.[66]

---

[64] Wermund, Benjamin, "Harmony charter chain agrees to changes after civil rights investigation," Houston Chronicle, November 26, 2014. Available at http://www.houstonchronicle.com/news/education/article/Harmony-charter-chain-agrees-to-changes-after-5920288.php See also this 22-page letter from the U.S. Department of Education Office for Civil Rights to the Superintendent of the TX Harmony Public Schools detailing its findings, resolution, and requirements for the Harmony Schools to come into compliance on federal non-discrimination regulations: http://www2.ed.gov/documents/press-releases/harmony-public-schools-letter.pdf
65 Kastner, Lindsay, "Auditors say funds misspent for Harmony campuses," My San Antonio, July 31, 2012. Available at http://www.mysanantonio.com/news/education/article/Auditors-say-funds-misspent-for-Harmony-campuses-3747674.php#ixzz22ahXPvXq
66 Stuart, Elizabeth, "Islamic links to Utah's Beehive Academy probed," Desert News, June 1, 2010. Available at http://www.deseretnews.com/article/700036619/Islamic-links-to-Utahs-Beehive-Academy-probed.html

Other Gulen Affiliates in the U.S.

Business, Banking, and Media

As noted above, the center of the Gulen Movement's power base long has been located in Turkey (although, as of late 2015, under serious pressure from Erdogan and the AKP government). Its network of wealthy Turks, both there and around the world, provides the massive donations that underwrite the Movement's global operations. Among these enterprises are banking, finance, insurance, media, and publishing interests. A representative listing may be found in Appendices C, D, E, and F below. For additional information, including a long list of corporations in the U.S. reportedly connected to the GM (as of January 2013), see the website of the Gulen watchdog organization, Turkish Invitations, at http://turkishinvitations.weebly.com/gulenist-corporations.html Such firms and their Gulenist connections form a close-knit network within which GM charter schools, cultural organizations, and other GM-linked groups are reported to channel their business preferentially to these companies.[67]

A key business arm of the GM is the Turkish Industrialists Confederation (TUSKON), an employers' organization located in Turkey that was formed in 2005 by seven business federations, comprising mostly small-to-medium sized businesses.[68] Originally favored by the Justice and Development Party (AKP), TUKSON was hard hit by the 2013-14 rift between Turkish President Recep Tayyip Erdogan and Fethullah Gulen. Trouble extended to TUSKON's premier bank, Bank Asia, which by April 2014, was facing serious government interference on its issuance of bond debt.[69] Bank Asia was taken over in mid-2015 by the Turkish state-run Savings Deposit Insurance Fund, which answers directly to the prime minister. Its top executives were dismissed and replacements named by the Turkish regime.[70] Reportedly as well, hundreds of Turkish businessmen have left the TUSKON confederation since it was targeted by the AKP.[71] On 6 November 2015, Ankara

---

67"Gulenist corporations," Turkish Invitations, available online at
http://turkishinvitations.weebly.com/gulenist-corporations.html
68 The Turkish language website of TUSKON may be found at http://www.tuskon.org/
69 Tremblay, Pinar, "Clash of the Anatolian Tigers," Al-Monitor, April 28, 2014. Available at
http://www.al-monitor.com/pulse/originals/2014/04/turkey-business-clash-gulen-akp.html
70 Peker, Emre, "Turkish Authorities Seize Bank Asya," Wall Street Journal, May 31, 2015. Available at
http://www.wsj.com/articles/turkish-authorities-seize-bank-asya-1433102306
71 Businessmen quit Gulen-affiliated organizations," Daily Sabah, April 30, 2014. Available at
http://www.dailysabah.com/economy/2014/05/01/businessmen-quit-gulenaffiliated-organizations

police raided TUSKON buildings in the Turkish capital, reportedly on orders of the Ankara Public Prosecutor's Office which was "investigating crimes against constitutional order."[72]

The GM Journalists and Writers Foundation (JWF), which invites foreign journalists to seminars on political topics, was founded in Istanbul in 1994 as a non-profit organization and generally serves as the Gülenists' unofficial public relations firm.[73] The JWF website (http://jwfglobal.org/) explains its mission as one of encouraging peaceful dialogue, freedom of speech, and social justice.[74] Its media affiliates, such as *Hizmet News*,[75] *Today's Zaman*,[76] and the *Cihan* News Agency,[77] however, work in concert to support the GM with favorable coverage and push back quickly to counter any moves against it. The JWF network reacted strongly, for example, to the Erdogan regime's heavy crackdown against the Gulen Movement in Turkey in 2015.

Notably, the JWF was granted general consultative status with the United Nations Economic and Social Council (ECOSOC) in 2012 and operates in many countries around the world, including Azerbaijan, Belarus, Estonia, Georgia, Kazakhstan, Kyrgyzstan, Moldova, the Russian Federation, Tajikistan, Turkey, Turkmenistan, and Ukraine. JWF additionally has contractual agreements with American newspapers, including the *Los Angeles Times* and *Washington Post*.

GM Cultural Centers: The Raindrop Turkish House

http://www.raindropturkishhouse.org/

The Raindrop Turkish House, or the Raindrop Foundation, founded by 'Turkish-Americans' in Houston, Texas in 2000, forms the hub of Gulen cultural activities in the U.S. and has expanded to include additional branches in five other states: Arkansas, Kansas, Mississippi, New Mexico, and Oklahoma. Its Houston complex houses several foundations, including the Turquoise Center and its Institute

---

72 "Ankara police raid Gülenist business confederation TUSKON over links with FETÖ terror organization," Daily Sabah, November 6, 2015. Available at
http://www.dailysabah.com/investigations/2015/11/06/ankara-police-raid-gulenist-business-confederation-tuskon-over-links-with-feto-terror-organization
73 Hansen, New Republic
74 Journalists and Writers Foundation, http://jwfglobal.org/
75 http://hizmetnews.com/
76 http://www.todayszaman.com/home
77 http://en.cihan.com.tr/en/

of Interfaith Dialog. The Turquoise Center, pictured below, was financed partly through donations from Gulen followers.[78]

Michael Stravato for *The New York Times*

At its website,[79] Raindrop notes that it hosts a wide range of cultural events, including the annual Turkish Language and Culture Olympiad, trips to Turkey every year, cultural and social events such as Turkish cuisine classes, cultural nights, *Nevruz* (New Year) picnics, traditional dinners, Turkish coffee nights, International Women's day, soccer games, Noah's pudding days, Whirling Dervishes' performances, and Intercultural Dialog Dinners. It hosts artistic exhibitions throughout the year and also offers Turkish and English classes, music courses, seminars and international conferences. Raindrop also helps the needy through its charity organization called "Helping Hands."[80]

A 2011 *New York Times* expose on the Gulen Movement claimed that "Dozens of Texans — from state lawmakers to congressional staff members to university professors — have taken trips to Turkey partly financed by the [Turquoise Center's] foundations" and added that the Raindrop Foundation had helped pay for State Senator Leticia Van de Putte's 2010 travel to Istanbul. In a troubling

RAINDR*P
FOUNDATION

[78] Saul
79 Raindrop Turkish House, http://www.raindropturkishhouse.org/about-raindrop
80 Ibid

indication of the kind of results such attention can achieve, her campaign report noted that in January 2011 she co-sponsored a Senate resolution commending Gulen for 'his ongoing and inspirational contributions to promoting global peace and understanding.'[81]

The Dialogue Institute of the Southwest (formerly known as the Institute of Interfaith Dialog) was noted above for its affiliation with the University of Houston. Established in 2002, the Institute promotes peace, harmony and the 'beauty of peaceful coexistence among Christians, Jews, and Muslims.' Aside from the usual trips to Turkey, the Institute also sponsors 'academic activities, grassroots-level activities such as luncheons and other get-togethers, and interfaith dinners involving diverse religious leaders.'[82]

Its website openly touts its affiliation with Fethullah Gulen and the Gulen Movement. Interfaith associations include the Arkansas Interfaith Alliance, Catholic Diocese of Little Rock, Congregation B'nai Israel, Faith Lutheran Church, First Presbyterian Church, Jewish Federation of Arkansas, Pulaski Heights United Methodist Church, UCA College of Liberal Arts as well as the Clinton Presidential Center in Little Rock, Arkansas. Oddly, although website photos picture individuals wearing the distinctive red and white hat associated with graduates of Sunni Islam's premier institute of higher learning, the Al-Azhar University in Cairo, Egypt, and testimonials from a gamut of Christian, Jewish and legislative figures, there is but one single named Muslim at the site: Imam Mustafa Yigit, an Al-Azhar graduate and Imam of the Houston Blue Mosque (aka Masjid al-Islam, originally a Nation of Islam mosque).[83] Yigit holds a Master's degree in Islamic Studies (Muslim-Christian Relations) from the Hartford Seminary at Hartford, Connecticut, which is closely affiliated with the Islamic Society of North America (ISNA), the largest Muslim Brotherhood front organization in the U.S. and an unindicted co-conspirator in the 2008 Holy Land HAMAS terror funding trial.[84]

---

81 Saul, New York Times
82 Dialogue Institute of the Southwest, http://www.interfaithdialog.org/
83 Ibid
84 Islamic Society of North America: An IPT Investigative Report, Investigative Project on Terrorism. Available at http://www.investigativeproject.org/documents/misc/275.pdf

Gulen on Gulen

While the large volume of information and reporting readily available about the Gulenist Movement is both useful and important, the heart of the Movement is the philosophy of Fethullah Gulen himself. Gulen has written voluminously over the years on a variety of topics. His philosophy, ideology, motivations and goals are important for Americans to understand primarily because of the movement's extensive and expanding presence in the U.S., particularly within the publicly-funded charter school system, but also in terms of its aggressive self-promotion through cultural organizations and open attempts to influence educators, legislators, and students with a worldview that is uncritically favorable towards both Islam and Turkey.

Especially because the majority of long-form literature about Gulen tends toward adulation, it is ever-more imperative that his own writing be examined under a careful light. Fethullah Gulen's official website[85] features many dozens of his essays on topics ranging from Thought, Faith, and Sufism, to Love and Tolerance. Among these, however, none is perhaps more revealing of Gulen's thinking than a book published in 1998 called *Prophet Mohammed as Commander.*[86] This book, therefore, is worth a closer examination at some length, as its themes validate much about the concerns with the Gulen Movement that have been discussed thus far here.

While much of the book details the life of Muhammad as a military commander and political leader, the opening sections of the book arguably reveal more about the author than they reveal about Muhammad, about whom much already has been written over the centuries. Following here, then, is a closer look at the first 37 pages of *Prophet Muhammad as Commander,* which contain some revealing passages in Gulen's own words and provide a window on his views about jihad and warfare.

In *Prophet Muhammad as Commander,* Gulen writes extensively about compassion:

- Muhammad's compassion

- The need for compassion

- What compassion means

---

[85] Fethullah Gulen, http://www.fgulen.com/en/
86 "Prophet Muhammad as Commander," http://www.fgulen.com/en/fethullah-gulens-works/1353-prophet-muhammad-as-commander

In three early passages of the book, however, Gulen defines compassion in ways that likely would seem jarring to the average Western reader:

> "The amputation of a gangrenous limb is an act of compassion to the rest of the whole body."

> "It is...of great importance to apportion the amount of compassion and to identify who deserves it."

> "God's Messenger, upon him be peace and blessings, says: Help your brother whether he be just or unjust. The Companions asked: 'How shall we help our unjust brother?' He replied: You help him by preventing him from doing injustice."

Obviously, Gulen is not talking about a Judeo-Christian perspective on compassion; rather, he is explaining the Islamic doctrine of 'enjoining the good and forbidding the evil.' That is, Gulen's definition of 'compassion' is not at all about extending empathy, sympathy, or feelings of care, concern or mercy towards another human being. He is a shariah-adherent Muslim, whose belief system relies on Qur'anic verses like the following:

> Allah, the Exalted, Says (what means): "Let there arise out of you a group of people inviting to all that is good (Islam), enjoining Al-Ma`roof (i.e., Islamic Monotheism and all that Islam orders one to do) and forbidding Al-Munkar (polytheism, disbelief and all that Islam has forbidden). And it is they who are the successful." [Quran 3:104]

And another is:

> "You (true believers in Islamic Monotheism) are the best of peoples ever raised up for mankind; you enjoin Al-Ma`roof (i.e., Islamic Monotheism and all that Islam has ordained) and forbid Al-Munkar (polytheism, disbelief and all that Islam has forbidden)". [Quran 3:110]

Thus, according to Gulen (whose understanding is accurately reflective of authoritative Islamic doctrine), Muhammad had no choice but to wage war against unbelievers as an act of compassion. This strongly suggests that "injustice" at the very least includes not believing in Allah (as Gulen alludes on page 4):

> "But what could he do for those who persisted in unbelief and actually waged war against him in order to destroy him and his Message? He had to fight against his enemies out of his universal compassion that encompasses every creature."

So again, according to Gulen, Muhammad waged war against unbelievers out of compassion. Given that all Muslims are obligated by the doctrine of their faith to strive to emulate Muhammad in all times and places, this message has serious implications for those who find themselves the global, and especially U.S., targets of the GM influence operation. Indeed, the following hadith from Sahih Muslim spells out the obligation of all Muslims who witness 'an evil' (under Islamic Law, or shariah) to do something about it—physically, if possible.

> Abu Sa`eed Al-Khudri, may Allah be pleased with him, reported: The Messenger of Allah, sallallaahu alayhi wa sallam, said, "Whoever amongst you sees an evil, he must change it with his hand; if he is unable to do so, then with his tongue; and if he is yet unable to do so, then with his heart; and that is the weakest form of Faith". [Sahih Muslim]

On page 6 of *Prophet Muhammad as Commander,* Gulen explains Muslim hostility toward non-Muslims who fail to acknowledge Allah and Muhammad in a similar manner, likewise redolent of Islamic supremacism:

> "For this reason, a Muslim's enmity towards unbelievers is, in fact, in the form of pitying them."

Failing to submit to the supremacy of Islam is the very definition of "injustice" in Islamic doctrine. Out of "compassion" for those unbelievers, but especially to prevent them from committing further injustice, Muslims are obligated to feel enmity towards them and to fight them as enemies.

Jihad as the core element of Islamic doctrine literally embodies justice. The section on Jihad in the Shafi'i book of Sacred Islamic Law, *Reliance of the Traveller* (*'Umdat al-Salik*),[87] is to be found in the Book of Justice (o9.0). Likewise, as Gulen accurately explains on page 20, Jihad is integral to justice:

> "God does not approve wrongdoing and disorder. He wills that human beings should live in peace and, accordingly, that justice should prevail amongst them. It is therefore incumbent upon those who believe in One God and worship Him faithfully to secure justice in the world. Islam calls this responsibility jihad."

Gulen then goes on to explain the various forms of jihad, including warfare. Again, on page 20, and in perfect accord with shariah, Gulen states the purpose of Jihad:

> "...to establish the supremacy of His religion and to make His Word prevail."

In the same section, Gulen then clearly references the Islamic doctrine of amr bi 'l-ma'ruf wa nahy an al-munkar and articulates the aim of establishing a worldwide caliphate:

> "Besides the holy struggle, the principle of amr bi 'l-ma'ruf wa nahy an al-munkar_(enjoining the good and forbidding the evil) seeks to convey the Message of Islam to all human beings in the world and to establish a model Islamic community on a world-wide basis."

Gulen does not distance himself in any way from the goal of establishing a worldwide caliphate. It is clear that he understands this is to be an obligatory objective for all Muslims.

Gulen next further identifies the two broad categories of jihad as the greater jihad and the lesser jihad. He describes the greater jihad as an internal spiritual struggle, and the lesser jihad as including warfare. It should be noted that this whole distinction between the so-called 'greater jihad' and 'lesser jihad', however, relies on a

---

[87] Reliance of the Traveller, The Classic Manual of Islamic Sacred Law ('Umdat al-Salik), d. 769/1368. Available at http://www.islamicbulletin.org/free_downloads/resources/reliance2_complete.pdf

weak hadith, transmitted through an unreliable chain of narrators. Whether sincerely or otherwise, Gulen here slips into an all-too-common pattern of de-emphasizing the importance of fighting in favor of a personal internal struggle. When he states on page 24, for example, that "only those who triumph over there carnal selves can perform the lesser jihad," he perpetuates an erroneous reversal of the actual importance of each in Islam.

Citing on the following page (page 25) the example of Muhammad, Gulen seems almost to try to rectify any prior misimpression by mentioning the 'two aspects of jihad' but then offering explicit praise of Muhammad for his battlefield prowess:

> "The Prophet, upon him be peace and blessings, combined these two aspects of jihad in the most perfect way in his person. He displayed monumental courage on battlefields."

Gulen goes on in the same vein, acknowledging truthfully that violent jihad is what resulted in the successful spread of Islam—not internal struggle to better oneself. He additionally identifies a broad set of circumstances in which Muslims should wage such jihad (page 27):

> "When the believers performed the lesser jihad whether by fighting on battlefields against those who waged war on them or tried to prevent them from worshipping One God only, or preaching the truth and enjoining the right and good and forbidding the wrong and evil, God's help and victory came, and men began to enter Islam in throngs."

So, as Gulen points out, violent jihad is not just waged against those who wage war against the believers. It is also waged against those who interfere with the spread and practice of Islam.

One of the most important sections (especially for non-Muslims) in *Prophet Muhammad as Commander* is on pages 29-31. It is here where Gulen defines the conditions under which Islam allows the use of force:

> "Islam seeks to call people with wisdom and fair exhortation, and does not resort to force until those who desire to maintain the corrupted order they built on injustice, oppression, self-interest and

exploitation of others and usurpation of their rights, resist it to prevent its preaching. Thus Islam allows the use of force in the following cases:

1. If unbelievers or polytheists or those who make mischief and corruption on the earth resist the preaching of Islam and try to block its way of conquering the minds and hearts of people. ...In case it is resisted or prevented, it offers its enemies three alternatives: either they will accept Islam, or allow its preaching or admit its rule. If they reject all three alternatives, Islam allows the use of force.

2. God permitted His Messenger to resort to the 'sword' only after he emigrated to Madina and established an independent state there. This permission was given because the Muslims were wronged.... It...has been witnessed by history, that Islam resorts to force in order to defend itself and establish freedom of belief...It is a historical fact which has been acknowledged even by many Western writers, that Christians and Jews have lived the most prosperous and happiest period of their history under the rule of Islam.

3. Islam...never approves any injustice in any part of the world...the righteous servants of God are charged with the duty of submitting the earth to God's rule, which depends on absolute justice and worship of only One God. They are also obliged to strive until persecution and the worship and obedience of false deities and unjust tyrants come to an end.

Thus, any society or civilization that is perceived to be standing in the way of or interfering with the spread of Islam is subject to lawful attack. Gulen's second point echoes the commonly-heard apologia that says virtually all violent Jihad is defensive. If Muslims are "wronged" they can wage violent jihad. As with a few other passages in this book, one wonders to what extent Gulen himself actually believes his next statement, that, in any case, Christians and Jews never had it so good as when conquered and ruled by Muslims. Gulen's final point here (3) is essentially a restatement of Qur'anic verse 8:39, which says

And fight them until there is no fitnah and [until] the religion, all of it, is for Allah . And if they cease - then indeed, Allah is Seeing of what they do.

As Gulen explains, because Muslims are tasked with subjugating the world to Islam, they are obligated to use whatever means necessary to accomplish the task, obviously including violent jihad.

Finally, on pages 31-37, Gulen provides what amount to rules for jihadis. Some are merely curiosities—others are ominous indeed.

> "So, whoever fights for other causes, such as fame or material gain, or for racial or other ideological considerations of similar nature, he will not be regarded as a fighter with whom God is pleased."

Here, Gulen seems to refer to Qur'anic admonishments like the following:

> Those who desire the life of the Present and its glitter, --to them we shall pay (the price of) their deeds therein,--without diminution. They are those for whom there is nothing in the Hereafter but the Fire: vain are the designs they frame therein, and of no effect are the deeds that they do! (Qur'an 11:15-16)

But he departs from scripture when he includes the additional prohibition of fighting for racial or other ideological considerations, which would seem to preclude fighting for a nation state or any leader motivated by racial or non-Islamic ideology.

Then Gulen returns to solid Islamic traditional ground with the following passages about the obligatory nature of violent jihad, the jihad of fighting and the battlefield:

> "Where fighting is necessary...the Quran exhorts believers not to avoid fighting."

> "When fighting is unavoidable, Muslims must not hesitate to take up arms and hasten to the front. The Qur'an exhorts Muslims to fight when necessary and severely reprimands those who show reluctance in mobilizing in the way of God..."

"One of the important points to be mentioned concerning jihad is that a believer cannot flee the battlefield."

"Fleeing on the battlefield is one of the seven major, perilous sins."

But the next passage, reminiscent at once of the Ayatollah Khomeini --

We do not worship Iran, we worship Allah. For patriotism is another name for paganism. I say let this land [Iran] burn. I say let this land go up in smoke, provided Islam emerges triumphant in the rest of the world.[88]

--and of Qur'anic verse 9:5 --

But when the forbidden months are past, then fight and slay the Pagans wherever ye find them, and seize them, beleaguer them, and lie in wait for them in every stratagem (of war)…

--is perhaps the most ominous of all for non-Muslims, in view of Iran's drive for deliverable nuclear weapons and the fact that a jihadist Pakistan already has them. Here Gulen says:

"…believers should also equip themselves with the most sophisticated weaponry. Force has an important place in obtaining the desired result, so believers cannot be indifferent to it. Rather they must be much more advanced in science and technology than unbelievers so that they should not allow unbelievers to use 'force' for their selfish benefit. According to Islam, 'right is might'; so, in order to prevent might from being right in the hands of unbelievers and oppressors, believers must be mightier than others."

"An Islamic state…should be able to secure peace and justice in the world and no power should have the courage to make corruption in any part of the earth. This will be possible when Muslims equip themselves with a strong belief and righteousness in all their affairs,

---

[88] Taheri, Amir, "Nest of Spies: America's Journey to Disaster in Iran (London: Hutchinson, 1988), p. 269. Available at http://www.amazon.com/Nest-Spies-Americas-Journey-Disaster/dp/0394575660

and also with scientific knowledge and the most sophisticated technology."

Similarly revealing of Gulen's close alignment with authoritative Islamic doctrine and law—as well as the never-directly-mentioned Muslim Brotherhood—is his commentary from the 'Reflections on the Quran' series. His brief comments on Surah 9 ('Tawbah') focus on Qur'anic verse 9:20, which reads as follows:

> "Those who believe and have emigrated (to the home of Islam in God's cause), and strive in God's cause with their wealth and persons are greater in rank in God's sight, and those are the ones who are the triumphant." (At-Tawbah 9:20)

For which Gulen's observations conclude with a summary of three obstacles that challenge faithful Muslims who seek Allah's favor by emulating Muhammad's original *Hijra* from Mecca to Medina but also "striving in order to exalt God's Word in the new land to which one has immigrated." Gulen's comment on Muslims who succeed in that challenge is both chilling and directly reminiscent of Brotherhood writing, including the "grand jihad" passage from the 'Explanatory Memorandum on the Strategic Goal for the Group in North America,'[89] and also sections of 'The Methodology of Dawah. As Gulen writes:'[90]

> Indeed, if "believing" means overcoming the first obstacle of Satan, "leaving one's tribe, community, and relatives in order to immigrate to a different land for the sake of belief" is surmounting another obstacle which is as powerful as the other. Without being content with leaving one's native land and relatives, "striving in order to exalt God's Word in the new land to which one has immigrated" **means destroying a third, great barrier.** One who has overcome all of these

---

[89] "Explanatory Memorandum on the Strategic Goals for the Group in North America," 5/22/1991. Available at http://www.investigativeproject.org/documents/misc/20.pdf
90 Siddiqi, Shamim A., "Methodology of Dawah." Available at http://www.dawahinamericas.com/bookspdf/MethodologyofDawah.pdf

obstacles or barriers has conquered his or her own carnal self and attained salvation.[91]

The Gulen Movement must be understood for the jihadist, subversive, worldwide Islamic network that it is. Just because Fethullah Gulen does not permit the revelation of any overt connections to the Muslim Brotherhood or other transnational jihad groups does not obviate their ideological synchrony. This is a dangerous organization that threatens Western civilization as surely as an al-Qa'eda or Islamic State—but with far greater finesse and stealth.

---

91 Fethullah Gulen's Works, 'Reflections on the Quran, Sūratu't-Tawbah (Repentance). Available at http://www.fgulen.com/en/fethullah-gulens-works/1283-reflections-on-the-quran/suratut-tawbah-repentance/33361-at-tawbah-9-20

Watchwords for the Gulen Movement: Awareness and Caution

With this monograph's admittedly brief look at the Gulen Movement, it must nevertheless be clear at this point that there is much more to this organization than at first meets the eye. The veil of ambiguity that shrouds the GM's jihadist agenda from genuine transparency is carefully maintained by an extended network of Gulenist-'inspired' supporters, whose global reach depends on substantial financial resources. This monograph has described some of the elements of the GM global empire, including academic, business, cultural, financial, and media assets. Ongoing U.S. federal investigations into widespread allegations about irregularities at the GM charter schools seem but the tip of the iceberg, as details about trip-funding scandals from local levels across the country but reaching even into the U.S. Congress have emerged. Additionally, the vicious Erdogan-Gulen power struggle in Turkey and Fethullah Gulen's own published writing on jihad both indicate that beneath the GM's carefully-cultivated façade of benign dedication to education, interfaith dialogue, peace, and tolerance lies a far more calculated agenda to promote Islam, jihad, and shariah worldwide.

Final Thoughts and Some Recommendations

There are several steps that Americans, including educators, federal officials, legislators, and parents can take to increase scrutiny of the Gulen Movement in the U.S. and to demand accountability from American elected officials, especially the administrative and teaching staff of GM charter schools and associated school boards.

1. Hold politicians accountable. When elected officials accept trips abroad that are sponsored and funded by the jihadist Gulen Movement, they need to hear from constituents—both through correspondence and in the voting booth. Demand that your elected members of Congress, your state legislature, your city council and others be aware of the GM campaign to influence them, conduct rigorous due diligence when they receive invitations that may be related to the GM, and refuse to attend GM events or to take these trips.

2. Demand that taxpayer-supported charter schools give priority to hiring American teachers and staff. If recruitment from abroad is absolutely necessary, then such schools must employ only non-discriminatory practices in both the hiring of teachers and the use of H-1B visas to bring in teachers from overseas. Some states have already moved to act in this direction with legislation.

3. School boards, administrators, and teachers involved with the GM charter school network have an obligation to familiarize themselves with the ideology of its founder, Fethullah Gulen, the history of the GM in Turkey, and the full extent of its presence in the U.S.

4. Become familiar with the wide range of Gulen Movement front groups, especially in the cultural area, so that events and invitations that at first glance may seem attractively benign are understood in the context of their Gulen connections

5. While Fethullah Gulen received Permanent Legal Resident (green card) status in 2008, should he apply for U.S. citizenship now that he is eligible, and even if he doesn't seek citizenship status, the Department of Homeland Security should undertake immediately a rigorous review of Gulen's suitability for legal status of any sort in the U.S.

6. The U.S. House of Representatives Homeland Security Committee and the Homeland Security and Governmental Affairs Committee in the Senate should hold joint hearings on the Gulen Movement, with a view to exposing not only the extent of its network in the U.S., but the jihadist ideology that inspires its founder and members

Appendix A: Publicly Funded Schools Currently in Operation

Source: http://turkishinvitations.weebly.com/list-of-us-schools.html

Arizona (7)

Management organization: Sonoran Schools

De facto management organization: Accord Institute for Education Research

Charter holder: Daisy Education Corporation*

1. Sonoran Science Academy - Tucson*:
   http://www.sonoranacademy.org/tucson/

2. Sonoran Science Academy – Broadway:
   http://www.sonoranacademy.org/broadway/

3. Sonoran Science Academy - Phoenix*:
   http://www.sonoranacademy.org/phoenix/

4. Sonoran Science Academy - Davis Monthan Air Force Base:
   http://www.sonoranacademy.org/davis-monthan/

5. Sonoran Science Academy – Ahwatukee*:
   http://www.sonoranacademy.org/ahwatukee/

6. Sonoran Science Academy – Peoria:
   http://www.sonoranschools.org/index.php/sonoran-schools/ssa-peoria

7. Paragon Science Academy: http://www.paragonscience.org/

Arkansas (2)

De facto management organization: Harmony Public Schools (formerly Cosmos Foundation): http://www.harmonytx.org

1. Lisa Academy http://www.lisaacademy.org/

2. Lisa Academy-North http://www.lisanorth.org/

California (11)

De facto management organization: Accord Institute for Education Research
Charter holder: Magnolia Foundation http://magnoliacharterschools.org/

1. Magnolia Science Academy 1 - Reseda
   http://reseda.magnoliascience.org/

2. Magnolia Science Academy 2 – Valley
   http://valley.magnoliascience.org/

3. Magnolia Science Academy 3 – Carson -
   http://gardena.magnoliascience.org/

4. Magnolia Science Academy 4 – Venice
   http://venice.magnoliascience.org/

5. Magnolia Science Academy 5 – Hollywood
   http://hollywood.magnoliascience.org/

6. Magnolia Science Academy 6 – Palms
   http://palms.magnoliascience.org/

7. Magnolia Science Academy 7 - Van Nuys
   http://vannuys.magnoliascience.org

8. Magnolia Science Academy 8 – Bell http://bell.magnoliascience.org/

9. Magnolia Science Academy - San Diego
   http://sandiego.magnoliascience.org/

10. Magnolia Science Academy – Santa Clara
    http://santaclara.magnoliascience.org

Charter holder: Willow Education

11. Bay Area Technology School (Oakland)
    http://www.baytechschool.org/j/index.php

Colorado (1)

De facto management organization: Accord Institute for Education Research

- Lotus School for Excellence – Aurora http://www.lotusschool.org/

District of Columbia (1)

Management organization: Harmony Public School (formerly Cosmos Foundation)

- Harmony D.C. — School of Excellence http://www.harmonydc.org

Florida (10)

Organization: Charter Educational Services & Resources http://charterresources.us formerly Grace Institute for Educational Research and Resources http://graceschools.us

1. Broward Math & Science Schools http://www.bmsschools.org/

2. Discovery Academy of Science http://www.discoveryacademy.info

3. New Springs Elementary School http://www.newspringsschools.org

4. New Springs Middle School http://newspringsschools.org/

5. Orlando Science Middle High School http://orlandoscience.org/

6. Orlando Science Elementary School http://orlandoscience.org/

7. River City Science Academy, Middle School
   http://www.rivercityscience.org/

8. River City Science Academy Innovation
   http://rivercityscience.org/innovation/

9. River City Science Elementary Academy
   http://rivercityscience.org/elementary

10. Stars Middle School, Tallahassee http://starsmiddleschool.org/

Georgia (2)

De facto management organization: Charter Educational Services & Resources http://charterresources.us formerly Grace Institute for Educational Research and Resources http://graceschools.us

- Fulton Science Academy High School (formerly TEACH-Technology Enriched Accelerated High) School http://fsahigh.org

- Fulton Sunshine Academy, Elementary School http://www.fultonsunshine.org/

Illinois (4)

Organization: Concept Schools http://www.conceptschools.org

1. Chicago Math and Science Academy http://cmsaonline.net

2. Horizon Science Academy Belmont http://www.hsabelmont.org

3. Horizon Science Academy McKinley Park http://www.hsamckinley.org

4. Quest Charter Academy http://www.questpeoria.org

Indiana (3)

Organization: Concept Schools, Inc. http://www.conceptschools.org

- Indiana Math and Science Academy – West http://www.imsaindy.org

- Indiana Math and Science Academy – North http://north.imsaindy.org

- Indiana Math and Science Academy – South
  http://south.imsaindy.org

Louisiana (1)

Charter holder : Pelican Educational Foundation

De facto management organization: Harmony Public Schools (formerly Cosmos Foundation) http://www.harmonytx.org

- Kenilworth Science and Technology, Baton Rouge
  http://www.kenilworthst.org

Maryland (4)

Charter holder: Chesapeake Lighthouse Foundation http://www.clfmd.org

De facto management organizations: Washington Educational Foundation http://www.weduf.org and Apple Educational Services

1. Chesapeake Math and IT Academy http://cmitacademy.org/

2. Chesapeake Math and IT Academy North aka CMIT Elementary http://cmitelementary.org/

3. Chesapeake Math and IT Academy South http://cmitsouth.org/

4. Chesapeake Science Point, Hanover http://www.mycsp.org/

Massachusetts (3)

De facto management organization: Apple Educational Services http://www.appleeducationalservices.org or http://aesny.org

- Pioneer Charter School of Science http://www.pioneercss.org

- Pioneer Charter School of Science II http://www.pioneercss.org

- Hampden Charter School of Science
  http://www.hampdencharter.org/

Michigan (1)

Management organization: Concept Schools http://www.conceptschools.org

- Michigan Math and Science Academy http://www.mmsaonline.org/

Minnesota (1)

Management organization: Concept Schools http://www.conceptschools.org

- Minnesota Math and Science Academy http://www.mmsaweb.org

Missouri (5)

Charter holder: Frontier Schools

De facto management organization: Harmony Public Schools (formerly Cosmos Foundation) http://www.harmonytx.org

1. Frontier School of Excellence a.k.a. Brookside-Frontier Math and Science School http://www.bfmass.org/ http://www.kcfse.org/

2. Frontier School of Innovation http://www.kcfsi.org/

3. Frontier STEM no website yet; see http://frontierschools.org

Management organization: Concept Schools http://www.conceptschools.org

4. Gateway Science Academy of St. Louis http://www.gsastl.org

5. Gateway Science Academy South http://www.gsasouth.org

Nevada (2)

Charter holder: Coral Education Corporation

De facto management organization: Accord Institute for Education Research

- Coral Academy of Science - Reno Elementary
  http://coralacademy.org/elementary/ Middle High
  http://www.coralacademy.org/middle http://www.coralacademy.org/high

- Coral Academy of Science - Las Vegas (legally a single school, but has 3 campuses with separate locations)
  http://www.coralacademylv.org/

New Jersey (6)

De facto management organization: Apple Educational Services or http://aesny.org

1. Central Jersey College Prep http://njcollegeprep.com/

2. Paterson Charter School For Science And Technology http://www.pcsst.org/

3. Thomas Edison Energy Smart Charter School http://energysmartschool.org

Organization: North Jersey Arts and Science Charter Schools http://njascs.org

4. Bergen Arts and Science Charter School (3 campuses) http://bergencharter.org

5. Passaic Arts and Science Charter School (2 campuses) http://passaiccharter.org/elementary/

6. Paterson Arts and Science Charter School http://www.pcsst.org

New Mexico (1)

De facto management organization: Cosmos Foundation/Harmony Public Schools

- Albuquerque School of Excellence http://www.abqse.org/

New York (4)

De facto management organization: Apple Educational Services http://www.appleeducationalservices.org or http://aesny.org

1. Syracuse Academy of Science http://www.sascs.org/

2. Buffalo Academy of Science http://www.bascs.org/

3. Rochester Academy Charter School http://www.rochester-academy.org/ and http://www.racschool.com/

4. Utica Academy of Science http://www.uascs.org

North Carolina (2)

De facto management organizations: Washington Educational Foundation http://www.weduf.org and Apple Educational Services

- Triad Math and Science Academy http://www.tmsacharter.org/

- Triangle Math and Science Academy http://tmsaacademy.org

Ohio (19)

Management organization: Concept Schools http://www.conceptschools.org

1. Horizon Science Academy Cincinnati http://www.horizoncincy.org/

2. Horizon Science Academy Cleveland http://www.hsas.org/

3. Horizon Science Academy Cleveland Middle School
   http://www.hsacms.org/

4. Horizon Science Academy Cleveland Elementary School
   http://es.horizoncleveland.org/

5. Horizon Science Academy Columbus High School
   http://www.horizoncolumbus.org/

6. Horizon Science Academy Columbus Middle School
   http://www.horizoncolumbus.org/ms/

7. Horizon Science Academy Columbus Elementary School
   http://es.horizoncolumbus.org/

8. Horizon Science Academy Dayton Elementary School
   http://es.horizondayton.org

9. Horizon Science Academy Dayton http://www.horizondayton.org/

10. Horizon Science Academy Dayton Downtown
    http://dt.horizontoledo.org

11. Horizon Science Academy Denison Middle School
    http://www.horizondenison.org/

12. Horizon Science Academy Denison Elementary School
    www.denisonelementary.org/

13. Horizon Science Academy Lorain http://www.horizonlorain.org/

14. Horizon Science Academy Springfield
    http://www.horizonspringfield.org/

15. Horizon Science Academy Toledo http://www.horizontoledo.org/

16. Horizon Science Academy Toledo Downtown
    http://dt.horizontoledo.org

17. Horizon Science Academy Youngstown
    http://www.horizonyoungstown.org/

18. Noble Academy-Columbus http://www.noblecolumbus.org/

19. Noble Academy-Cleveland http://www.noblecleveland.org/

Oklahoma (4)

Charter holder: Sky Foundation

De facto management organization: Harmony Public Schools (formerly Cosmos Foundation) http://www.harmonytx.org

1. Discovery School of Tulsa http://www.discoveryok.org/

2. Dove Science Academy- Oklahoma City http://www.dsaokc.org/

3. Dove Science Academy Elementary School http://www.dsaelementary.org/

4. Dove Science Academy-Tulsa http://dsatulsa.org/

Pennsylvania (3)

De facto management organization: Apple Educational Services http://www.appleeducationalservices.org or http://aesny.org

• Truebright Science Academy, Philadelphia http://www.truebright.org/

• Young Scholars of Central Pennsylvania http://www.yscp.org/

• Young Scholars of Western Pennsylvania http://www.yswpcs.org/

South Carolina (1)

• Greenville Renewable Energy Education ("GREEN") Charter School http://www.scgreencharter.org/

Tennessee (1)

De facto management organization: Harmony Public Schools (formerly Cosmos Foundation) http://www.harmonytx.org

- Memphis School of Excellence http://www.sememphis.org/

Texas (45)

Charter holder/Management Organization: Harmony Public Schools (formerly Cosmos Foundation) http://www.harmonytx.org

Austin area

1. Harmony School of Science – Austin http://hssaustin.org/

2. Harmony Science Academy - North Austin http://hsana.org/

3. Harmony School of Excellence – Austin http://hseaustin.org/

4. Harmony Science Academy - Austin http://hsaaustin.org/

5. Harmony School of Political Science and Communication http://hspaustin.org

Brownsville

6. Harmony Science Academy - Brownsville http://hsabrownsville.org/

Dallas area

7. Harmony Science Academy - Waco http://hsawaco.org/

8. Harmony Science Academy - Garland http://hsagarland.org/

9. Harmony Science Academy - Dallas http://hsadallas.org Elementary http://hsedallas.org Middle School http://hsmdallas.org

10. Harmony School of Innovation - Dallas (formerly Harmony School of Innovation Carrollton) http://hsacarrollton.org/

11. Harmony School of Business http://hsbdallas.org

El Paso

12. Harmony Science Academy - El Paso http://hsaelpaso.org/

13. Harmony School of Innovation - El Paso http://hsielpaso.org/

Fort Worth area

14. Harmony Science Academy - Fort Worth http://hsafortworth.org/

15. Harmony School of Innovation - Fort Worth
http://hsifortworth.org

16. Harmony Science Academy - Grand Prairie http://hsagp.org/

17. Harmony Science Academy – Euless http://hsaeuless.org/

18. Harmony School of Nature and Athletics – Dallas
http://hsnature.org/

19. Harmony School of Innovation Euless http://www.hsieuless.org

Houston north area

20. Harmony School of Endeavor – Houston
http://hsendeavor.org/default.asp

21. Harmony Science Academy - Bryan/College Station
http://hsabcs.org/

22. Harmony Science Academy - Houston Northwest http://hsanw.org/

23. Harmony School of Excellence - Houston http://hsehouston.org/

24. Harmony School of Advancement High http://hsadvancement.org/

25. Harmony School of Discovery http://hsdhouston.org/

26. Harmony School of Exploration http://www.hehouston.org

Houston south area

27. Harmony School of Ingenuity http://hsingenuity.org/default.asp

28. Harmony Science Academy - Beaumont http://hsabeaumont.org/

29. Harmony Science Academy - Houston
http://hsahouston.org/default.asp

30. Harmony Science Academy High School - Houston
http://hshigh.org/

31. Harmony School of Innovation - Houston
http://hsihouston.org/default.asp

32. Harmony School of Art (and Technology) – Houston
http://hsart.org

Houston west area

33. Harmony School of Science - Houston http://hsshouston.org/

34. Harmony Science Academy - West Houston http://hsawh.org

35. Harmony School of Science High – Sugarland http://hsshigh.org

Laredo

36. Harmony Science Academy – Laredo http://hsalaredo.org/

37. Harmony School of Innovation – Laredo http://hsilaredo.org

Lubbock area

38. Harmony Science Academy – Lubbock http://hsalubbock.org/

39. Harmony Science Academy – Odessa http://hsaodessa.org/

San Antonio area

40. Harmony Science Academy - San Antonio http://hsasa.org/

41. Harmony School of Innovation - San Antonio http://hsisa.org/

Charter holder: SST Schools (formerly Riverwalk Education Foundation, Inc.) http://www.ssttx.org/

De facto management Organization: Harmony Public Schools (formerly Cosmos Foundation) http://www.harmonytx.org

42. School of Science and Technology Discovery - Leon Valley
     http://www.sstdiscovery.org/

43. School of Science and Technology - San Antonio
     http://www.ssttx.org/default.asp

44. School of Science and Technology - Corpus Christi
     http://www.sstcc.org/

45. School of Science and Technology – Alamo
     http://www.sstalamo.org/default.asp

Utah (1)

De facto management organization: Accord Institute for Education Research

- Beehive Science and Technology Academy
  http://www.beehiveacademy.org

Wisconsin (1)

Management organization: Concept Schools

- Milwaukee Math and Science Academy
  http://www.mmsacademy.org/

Schools closed or removed from Gulenist control

California (3)

- Magnolia Science Academy - San Diego 2
  http://sandiego2.magnoliascience.org/

- Pacific Technology School – Orangevale http://ov.ptscharter.org/

- Pacific Technology School Santa Ana (a.k.a. PTS Orange County
  http://oc.ptscharter.org/) [statewide benefit charter not renewed; new
  charter approved to reopen as Magnolia Science Academy Santa
  Ana]

Florida (1)

- Sweetwater Branch Academy, Middle School, Gainesville
  http://swbacademy.org/

Georgia (1)

- Fulton Science Academy Middle School
  http://www.fultonscience.org/

Louisiana (1)

- Abramson Science and Technology, New Orleans
  http://www.abramsonst.org/

Maryland (1)

- Baltimore IT Academy http://www.bitacademy.org/

Minnesota (1)

Management organization: Concept Schools

- Minnesota School of Science http://www.mssonline.org/

Wisconsin (1)

- Wisconsin Career Academy http://wiscca.org

Appendix B: Gulen Movement Universities

Source: http://turkishinvitations.weebly.com/every-continent-but-antarctica.html

Albania

- Beder University www.beder.edu.al

- Epoka University www.epoka.edu.al

Bosnia

- International Burch University www.ibu.edu.ba

Cyprus

- Eastern Mediterranean University www.emu.edu.tr

Macedonia

- International Balkan University www.ibu.edu.mk

Montenegro

- Mediterranean University www.unimediteran.net

Romania

- University of Southeast Europe / Lumina University www.lumina.org

Turkey

- Antalya International University www.antalya.edu.tr

- Gediz University www.gediz.edu.tr

- Fatih University www.fatih.edu.tr

- Meliksah University www.meliksah.edu.tr

- Mevlana University www.mevlana.edu.tr

- Zirve University www.zirve.edu.tr

USA

- Fairfax, Virginia: Virginia International University www.viu.edu

- Illinois: American Islamic College www.aicusa.edu

- Houston, Texas: North American University www.northamerican.edu

Appendix C: The Gulen Movement Media Empire

Media

- The Journalists and Writers Foundation (JWF) http://jwfglobal.org/

- Hizmet News http://hizmetnews.com/

- Today's Zaman ('Time') http://www.todayszaman.com/home
  İstanbul, Turkey

- Samanyolu TV (Milky Way Publishing Services Inc.)
  http://www.samanyolu.tv/hakkinda

Samanyolu ('Galaxy') TV is an online streaming service and international media corporation with offices in Azerbaijan, Germany, Turkey and the U.S.

Ebru TV is a cable TV network majority owned by the Gulenist Samanyolu Broadcasting Company. Available on RCN basic cable in Manhattan, NY, Washington, D.C., Boston, Chicago, Lehigh Valley and Philadelphia as well as the Globecast World TV. U.S. headquarters is located at 300 Franklin Square Dr., Somerset, NJ.

- Ebru TV ('Marbling, watering') http://ebru.tv/

Mehtap ('Moonlight') is a website that streams TV shows, radio programs, and different series. Shows include "Family Guide," "Fethullah Gulen | Hercules Tunes," "Hadith Reading," and "Islam and Life." Headquarters located in Uskudar, Istanbul, Turkey

- Mehtap (Moonlight) TV http://www.mehtap.tv/

- Cihan ('Universe') News Agency http://en.cihan.com.tr/en/ Istanbul,
  Turkey

Founded in 1993, published bimonthly in the U.S., and distributed throughout the world, **The Fountain** covers themes on life, belief, knowledge, and universe, including writings by Fethullah Gulen. The magazine is published by Tughra Books, the Gulen publishing house.

Headquartered in Rutherford, New Jersey, U.S. but with offices in Cairo, Istanbul, Kuala Lumpur, Moscow, and Sydney

- The Fountain Magazine (http://www.fountainmagazine.com/)

The Blue Dome is a Gulen publishing house headquartered in Clifton, NJ. Focus is on academic works in the fields of interfaith dialogue, intercultural studies, art, and history. Turkish authors predominate but Georgetown's John Esposito is also featured.

- The Blue Dome Press http://www.bluedomepress.com/

Tughra Books is a Gulen publishing house with its main office in Clifton, NJ that publishes books on Islam, Islamic history and art, and Islamic spirituality and traditions. Turkish authors predominate and Fethullah Gulen is a featured writer. Also has an office in Istanbul, Turkey

- Tughra Books (formerly The Light Publishing, Inc.) http://www.tughrabooks.com/

Appendix D: Gulen Movement Business Affiliates

1. Bank Asya

   Ümraniye, Istanbul, Turkey

   http://www.bankasya.com.tr/en/default.aspx

   (Taken over mid-2015 by Erdogan AKP regime)

2. Isik Sigorta (insurance company)

   http://www.isiksigorta.com/

   Ümraniye, Istanbul, Turkey

   Isik Sigorta ('Light Insurance') is an insurance company that offers fire insurance, green card insurance, auto accident insurance, agriculture insurance, and health insurance. The majority of its shares are controlled by Bank Asya (listed above).

3. Turkish Confederation of Businessmen and Industrialists

   http://www.tuskon.org

   Headquarters located in Istanbul, Turkey but with offices also in Beijing, Moscow, Brussels, and Washington, D.C.

4. Koza Ipek Holding

   http://www.kozaipekholding.com/

   Turkish business conglomerate founded in 1948 but now considered affiliated with the Gulen Movement. Group includes media, mining, and printing companies. 20 of its media holdings were raided by Turkish government police on 1 September 2015. Placed under court-ordered panel of trustees in late October 2015. Koza Ipek media group in Istanbul stormed by police 28 October 2015.

Appendix E: Gulen Movement Think-Tanks and Cultural Organizations

1. Rumi Forum

http://rumiforum.org/

Founded in 1999, the Rumi Forum sponsors conferences, panel discussions, 'community engagement, luncheons, publications, scholarships, and other activities' to 'foster intercultural dialogue, stimulate thinking and exchange of opinions' on issues including 'pluralism, peace building and conflict resolution, intercultural and interfaith dialogue, social harmony and justice, civil rights and community cohesion,' according to its website.

The honorary president is Fethullah Gulen.

Headquarters location at 750 First St NE #1120, Washington, DC 20002 with local chapters in Maryland, Kentucky, Delaware, North Carolina, and Virginia

2. Alliance for Shared Values

http://www.afsv.org/

Openly affiliated with the GM at its website, the Alliance for Shared Values is an umbrella non-profit organization whose member organizations are 'founded by individuals who are participants in the *Hizmet* social initiative,' according to the group's website.

Member groups include:

- The Atlantic Institute

- The Rumi Forum

- The Pacifica Institute

- The Dialogue Institute Southwest

- The Niagara Foundation

- The Peace Islands Institute .

Groups are committed to promoting community service, social justice, education, and interfaith and intercultural dialogue.

3. Niagara Foundation

http://www.niagarafoundation.org/

Fethullah Gulen is honorary President. "Niagara Foundation strives to promote social cohesion by fostering civic conversations and sustained relationships between people of different cultures and faiths."

Location: Chicago, Illinois

Appendix F: The Gulen Movement's Turkic American Alliance

http://turkicamericanalliance.org/

Founded at a lavish event at the Willard Hotel in Washington, DC in May 2010 as 'The Assembly of Turkic American Foundations.' The Turkey-based English language daily, *Hurriyet Daily News,* reported that six Turkish-American federations 'which have a close proximity to Mr. Fethullah Gulen' joined together with a half-dozen U.S. Senators and a few dozen Representatives to celebrate the new organization.[92]

Citing the GM's typical operational caution, the article expresses surprise at Gulen's 'sudden and unexpected decision to combine all of their 180 cultural organizations under one umbrella assembly' in such a public way. The reference to '180 organizations' does not include the network of Gulen schools in the U.S. (although a couple are listed below), but primarily represents its cultural and non-governmental organizations (NGOs). The GM success in attracting such a significant attendance from among U.S. Congressional members at this `inaugural event signaled a new and more aggressive phase for the GM in terms of seeking to attract favorable attention from federal-level legislators.

The Turkic American Alliance website (http://turkicamericanalliance.org/) shows links to its six member groups:

1. Council of Turkic American Associations
    (http://turkicamericanalliance.org/ctaa/)

---

[92] Tanir, Ilhan, "The Gulen movement plays big in Washington," *Al-Hurriyet Daily News,* 5/14/2010. Available at http://www.hurriyetdailynews.com/default.aspx?pageid=438&n=the-gulen-movement-plays-big-in-washington-2010-05-14 See also the Gulen watchdog website at http://turkishinvitations.weebly.com/turkic-american-alliance-member-organizations.html

2. Turkic American Federation of Midwest
    (http://turkicamericanalliance.org/members/tafm/)

3. Turkic American Federation of Southeast
    (http://turkicamericanalliance.org/tafs-atlanta/)

4. Turquoise Council of Americans and Eurasians
    (http://turkicamericanalliance.org/tcae-houston/)

5. The West America Turkic Council
    (http://turkicamericanalliance.org/watc-los-angeles/)

Appendix G: Turkic American Alliance Subgroups

http://turkicamericanalliance.org/
(Drawn from their combined websites, April 2011)

Council of Turkic American Associations (40)

http://www.turkiccouncil.org/

The TAA website says "CTAA represents 43 member organizations in 9 states from Pennsylvania to Maine." Together, the lists of member organizations shown on the TAA and CTAA websites indicate only 40. It is unclear what the additional 3 organizations are, and why they are not mentioned on the websites.

New York (21)

1. Turkish Cultural Center New York
   http://www.turkishculturalcenter.org

2. Turkish Cultural Center of Staten Island http://www.tccsi.org

3. Turkish Cultural Center Brooklyn http://www.tccbrooklyn.org

4. Turkish Cultural Center Queens http://www.tccqueens.org

5. Turkish Cultural Center Syracuse http://www.tccsyr.org

6. Turkish Cultural Center Buffalo http://www.tccbuffalo.org

7. Turkish Cultural Center Rochester http://www.tccrochester.com

8. Turkish Cultural Center Ithaca http://www.tccithaca.org

9. Turkish Cultural Center Albany http://www.tccalbany.org

10. Turkish Cultural Center Long Island http://www.tccli.com

11. Turkish Cultural Center Binghamton
   http://www.tccbinghampton.org

12. Turkish Cultural Center Westchester http://www.tccwestchester.net

13. Turkish American Business Improvement & Development Council
   - New York http://www.tabid.org

14. TABID Queens

15. TABID Brooklyn

16. TABID Staten Island

17. TABID Westchester

18. TABID Long Island

19. TABID Manhattan

20. Universal Foundation http://www.universalfoundationny.org/

21. Brooklyn Amity School (logo is shown on TAA site under CTAA,
   yet for reasons unclear it is not listed as a member organization on
   the CTAA site itself) http://www.amityschool.org/

New Jersey (8)

1. Turkish Cultural Center New Jersey www.tccnj.org

2. Turkish Cultural Center of Central Jersey www.tccnj.org

3. Turkish Cultural Center of South Jersey www.tccsj.com

4. Interfaith Dialog Center www.idcnj.org

5. Pioneer Academy of Science www.pioneeracademy.org

6. Milky Way Education Center

7. TABID (Turkish American Business Improvement &Development Council) New Jersey

8. TABID South Jersey

Connecticut (3)

1. Turkish Cultural Center Connecticut
   http://www.TurkishCulturalCenterCt.com

2. Putnam Science Academy http://www.putnamscience.org

3. Turkish American Business Improvement & Development Council - TABID CT

Massachusetts (3)

1. Turkish Cultural Center Boston
   http://www.turkishcenterboston.org

2. Turkish Cultural Center Western Massachusetts
   http://www.tccwesternmass.org

3. Turkish American Business Improvement & Development Council - TABID MA

Pennsylvania (5)

1. Dialogue Forum www.dialogueforum.us/

2. Red Rose Foundation http://www.redrosefoundation.org

3. Turkish Cultural Center Pittsburgh http://tccpittsburgh.org/

4. Lehigh Dialogue Center http://lehighdialogue.org

5. Turkish American Business Improvement & Development Council Pennsylvania

MAFTAA – Mid-Atlantic Federation of Turkic American Associations (17)

http://maftaa.org/

1. Rumi Forum Washington DC http://www.rumiforum.org/

2. ATCCR, American Turkish Cultural Center Richmond http://www.richmondtogether.com/

3. American Turkish Cultural Center Charlottesville

4. ATFA, American Turkish Friendship Association, Virginia http://www.atfa.us

5. ATFA, American Turkish Friendship Association, West Virginia

6. ATFA, American Turkish Friendship Association, Delaware http://www.atfade.org/

7. Turkuaz Foundation Hampton Road(s) http://turkuazfoundation.com

8. Institute of Islamic-Turkish Studies Virginia http://www.iitstudies.org/

9. TACTIC DC, Turkish American Chamber of Trade Industry and Commerce (shown on TAA site as MAFTAA member, but not on MAFTAA website member list)

10. MARTI, Maryland Turkish American Inhabitants

11. Divan Center, North Carolina http://www.divancenter.org/ (There is also a Gulenist Divan Cultural Center at Triad http://www.divantriad.org/ but it is not shown as a MAFTAA member.)

12. Prospect Foundation Kentucky

13. DATCEF, Delaware American Turkish Cultural & Educational Foundation

14. Pinnacle Academy, Virginia (shown on TAA site as MAFTAA member, but not on MAFTAA website member list) http://pinnacleacademyva.com/

15. Society of American Turkish Academicians

16. Azerbaijani-American Cultural Association

17. Eurasian American Cultural Association

Turkish American Federation of Midwest (41)

http://www.turkishfederation.org/

Illinois

1. Turkish American Society of Chicago (TASC)

2. Niagara Foundation

3. Islamic Society of Chicago

4. Chicago Turkish American Chamber of Commerce (CTACC)

5. Ahiska Turks Cultural Center

6. Science Academy of Chicago (SAC) (also using name Science Academy Private School with name change on logo)

7. Kyrgyz American Association

8. Turkmen American Student Organization

9. Turkish American Academics of Midwest

Indiana

1. Niagara Foundation Indianapolis

2. Niagara Foundation Lafayette

3. Niagara Foundation Bloomington

4. Turkish American Society of Indiana

Iowa

1. Iowa Dialog Center

2. Niagara Foundation Des Moines

3. Turkish American Society of Iowa

Michigan

1. Niagara Foundation Detroit

2. Niagara Foundation Lansing

3. Turkish American Society of Michigan

4. Bosnian American Great Lakes Society of Friendship and Culture

Minnesota

1. Northern Lights Society

2. Niagara Foundation Minneapolis

3. Turkish American Society of Minnesota

Missouri

1. Niagara Foundation St. Louis

2. Turkish American Society of Missouri - http://tasom.org/

Nebraska

1. Niagara Foundation Omaha

2.   Niagara Foundation Lincoln

3.   Tajik American Association

Ohio

Only 7 organizations are shown on the TAFM website; 3 branches of the Turkish American Society of Ohio are shown, one with unspecified location, and the Columbus and Cleveland branches. However, Turkish American Society of Ohio has 5 known branches; it is presumed here that the Dayton, Central Ohio and Northern Ohio branches are also members of TAFM even though the TAFM website does not indicate this.

1.   Scioto Educational Foundation http://www.sefohio.org/

2.   Niagara Foundation Columbus
     http://columbus.niagarafoundation.org/

3.   Niagara Foundation Cleveland

4.   Niagara Foundation Toledo

5.   Turkish American Society of Central Ohio http://www.taaco.org/

6.   Turkish American Society of Northern Ohio http://www.taaco.org/

7.   Turkish American Society of Ohio Dayton
     http://www.tasodayton.org/

8.   Turkish American Society of Ohio Columbus
     http://tasocolumbus.org

9.   Turkish American Society of Ohio Cleveland
     http://www.tasocleveland.org/

Wisconsin

1.   Niagara Foundation Madison

2. Niagara Foundation Milwaukee

3. Harmony Foundation

4. Madison Turkish American Culture Center
   http://www.taccmadison.org

TAFS - Turkish American Federation of Southeast (8)

The TAA website says "Turkish American Federation of Southeast (TAFS) is a newly established federation whose members consist of Turkish and Turkic organizations in Georgia, Florida, South Carolina, Alabama, and Tennessee and has 22 members throughout the southeast." However, the TAA site shows logos for only 8 organizations, and the TAFS website gives no membership information whatsoever. The identity of the other 14 member entities is unknown.

1. Istanbul Center http://www.istanbulcenter.org/

2. Knoxville Turkish Cultural Center http://knoxvilleturkish.org/

3. Orlando Turkish Cultural Center a.k.a. Orlando Culture and Dialog Center Inc. aka Nile Foundation http://www.nilefoundation.com/

4. Turkish Cultural Center Tampa Bay http://www.tampaturkish.org

5. Anatolia Cultural Center http://www.anatoliacenter.org/

6. Peace Valley Foundation http://www.peacevalleyfoundation.org/

7. TACC (Turkish American Chamber of Commerce of Southeast) http://www.taccsoutheast.com/

8. SUD – Society of Universal Dialogue http://www.universaldialog.org/

http://www.tcae.org/

A number of organizations are no longer shown as members on the website of the TCAE, yet their logos are still shown on the TAA website. The following list combines the TCAE members shown on both the TCAE and TAA sites.

1. The Institute of Interfaith Dialog http://www.interfaithdialog.org/

2. Raindrop Turkish House Austin
    http://www.raindropturkishhouse.org/austin

3. Raindrop Turkish House College Station
    http://www.raindropturkishhouse.org/collegestation

4. Raindrop Turkish House Dallas
    http://www.raindropturkishhouse.org/dallas

5. Raindrop Turkish House El Paso
    http://www.raindropturkishhouse.org/elpaso

6. Raindrop Turkish House Houston (Bellfort Ave.)
    http://www.raindropturkishhouse.org/

7. Raindrop Turkish House Houston (Kinghurst St)

8. Raindrop Turkish House Lubbock
    http://www.raindropturkevi.org/lubbock/

9. Raindrop Turkish House San Antonio
    http://www.raindropturkishhouse.org/sanantonio

10. TTACC (Texas Turkish American Chamber of Commerce)
    http://www.ttacc.org/

11. Shanyraq Kazakh Foundation http://shanyraq.org/

12. Atlas Foundation http://www.atlaslouisiana.org/

13. Azerbaijanian American Cultural Alliance
    http://www.aacalliance.com/

14. Bosniaks Cultural Community of Houston

15. Bluebonnet Learning Center
    http://www.bluebonnetlearningcenter.com/

16. Turkmen Young Scholars Association

17. Raindrop Helping Hands http://raindropturkevi.org/helpinghands/

18. Turkish American Women Association http://tawadallas.org/

19. Citadel, aka Houston Blue Mosque
    http://www.houstonbluemosque.org/

West American Turkic Council (18)

http://www.watc.org/

The TAA website says that "West American Turkic Council (WATC) is serving 21 affiliate organizations representing 12 states in the West..." However, the WATC website shows only 18 member organizations. The identity of the remaining 3 member entities remains unknown.

Arizona (2)

1. Foundation for Intercultural Dialog FID http://www.fid-az.org/

2. Sema Foundation http://semafoundation.org/

California (8)

1. Pacifica Institute - Orange County http:/www.pacificainstitute.org

2. Pacifica Institute – Los Angeles

3. Pacifica Institute – San Diego

4. Pacifica Institute – Silicon Valley

5. Pacifica Institute – Sacramento

6. Tolerance Foundation http://www.tolerancefoundation.org

7. CATA Chamber http://www.catachamber.org

8. BAYCC http://baycc.org

Colorado (2)

1. Mosaic Foundation http://www.mosaicfoundation.org/

2. CO-TA http://www.co-ta.org/

Nevada (2)

1. Sierra Foundation http://www.sierraf.org/

2. Pacifica Institute – Las Vegas

Oregon (1)

1. Rosegarden http://rosegardencc.org

Utah (1)

1. Pacifica Institute-Utah dba Multicultural Arch Foundation

Washington (2)

1. Acacia Foundation http://www.acaciafoundation.org/

2. NOWTA http://www.nowta.org

Appendix H: Other Gulen Movement Charities and NGOs

1. Kimse Yok Mu

http://www.kimseyokmu.org.tr/?lang=en

"Kimse Yok Mu ('Is anyone there?') is an international non-profit humanitarian aid and development organization based in Turkey with 31 branches throughout the country which also provides humanitarian relief in over 113 countries"

"Some of the fields KYM is involved in are education, social services, medical services, housing, disaster relief, emergency response, sustainable development as well as providing food aid, basic necessities, and household goods."

Location: Turkey (with various branches around Turkey)

http://map.kimseyokmu.org.tr/ (link to locations)

2. Helping Hand for Relief and Development

http://www.hhrd.org/Default

Influenced by Gulen. "HHRD was founded in 2005 upon the Islamic Principle illustrated in the Gracious Quran: 'They feed with food--despite their own desire for it-- the indigent, and the orphan and the captive (saying): 'We feed you purely for the sake of God. We desire no reward from you, nor thankfulness.' - Surah al-Insan 8-9"

Mission Statement: "HHRD is committed to serve humanity by integrating resources for people in need. We strive to provide immediate response in disasters, and effective Programs in places of suffering, for the pleasure of Allah."

"In 2012, ICNA Relief USA received a $30,000 grant from none other than Helping Hand for Relief and Development, a Michigan-based Islamic charity with links to a Pakistani front charity that funds HAMAS. In 2006, the Pakistani charity Al-Khidmat Foundation gave a 6 million rupee check to HAMAS leader Khaled Meshaal."

http://counterjihadreport.com/tag/andre-carson/

"Charity Navigator does not appear to have factored in Helping Hand's ongoing cooperation (see here and here) with the Al-Khidmat Foundation, a

Pakistani charity which gave a 6 million rupee check to Hamas leader Khaled Meshaal in 2006."

Location: Detroit, Michigan

https://moneyjihad.wordpress.com/2013/09/12/helping-hand-
honored-despite-close-ties-to-a-hamas-funding-pakistani-charity/